Speak Up! Christian Assertiveness

Speak Up!
Christian Assertiveness

Randolph K. Sanders
and H. Newton Malony

The Westminster Press
Philadelphia

Scripture quotations are from *Good News Bible: The Bible in Today's English Version.* Old Testament: © American Bible Society, 1976; New Testament: © American Bible Society, 1966, 1971, 1976.

Book design by Gene Harris

First edition

Published by The Westminster Press®
Philadelphia, Pennsylvania

PRINTED IN THE UNITED STATES OF AMERICA
9 8 7 6 5 4 3 2 1

Library of Congress Cataloging in Publication Data

Sanders, Randolph K.
    Speak up! Christian assertiveness.

    Bibliography: p.
    1. Assertiveness (Psychology)—Religious aspects—Christianity. 2. Christian life—1960– . I. Malony, H. Newton. II. Title.
BV4647.A78S26   1985   248.4   84-20806
ISBN 0-664-24551-X (pbk.)

Contents

Preface	7
How to Use This Book	9
1: My Tongue Hurts	11
2: Powder Kegs, Cream Puffs, and Things in Between	15
3: A Message from God: "Speak Up!"	25
4: Talking to Yourself: The First Step	33
5: How to Be Assertive (And Courteous Too!)	47
6: Assertiveness in Everyday Life	59
7: One Month to Greater Assertiveness	81
8: Being Assertive in the Midst of Conflict	89
9: Being Assertive at Church	99
The Last Word	111
Appendixes	113
Notes	115
Further Reading	117

Preface

This book comes out of a number of years of research and clinical practice. It also comes out of personal experience.

Like many other people, we grew up with the misconception that there were only two ways to communicate through conflict: the aggressive way or the passive way. Neither way seemed to be very effective for resolving conflict, and both often led to disappointment. Fortunately, over time, we learned that being assertive represents a positive alternative to acting like a "tiger" or a "doormat." This book explains how.

Like any other book of this type, this volume is designed to provide information and education. It is not designed to take the place of psychological, medical, or other individualized professional services.

Many people help to make a book a reality. It would be impossible for us to name everyone. Our wives, Bette Sanders and Suzanna Malony, have been sources of love and support throughout.

Our appreciation goes to Kathy Carder for typing the bulk of the manuscript. We also thank the research assistants, our colleagues, and many others who contributed their time and skill. Thanks also go to the people at Westminster who put the material together into a finished product.

RANDOLPH K. SANDERS
H. NEWTON MALONY

How to Use This Book

There are many different kinds of books. This is a how-to book. Our purpose is to help you learn to communicate more effectively and appropriately in your daily life.

Just reading this book will make little difference in your ability to communicate. You have to take action on the ideas expressed in the pages that follow. That's why we've included a number of written exercises to challenge you to act on what you learn here. To get maximum benefit, resolve now to do the exercises. Set aside a special notebook for them.

We also encourage you to invite a friend to read the book as you do and go through the exercises with you. Pick someone who supports and cares about you, someone you think will benefit from reading the book too. Using this buddy system is not absolutely necessary, but it will help substantially. Communicating assertively is an interpersonal skill. If you are to use this skill well, you will have to spend time learning it in interpersonal situations. The buddy system will help you do this.

If you feel hesitant about asking someone to read the book with you, don't be surprised. Many people experience this. For some it's because they are afraid of imposing on others or because they think others may not need help. Whatever the reason, we encourage you to push yourself to find a buddy to help you. You'll be surprised to discover that many people have difficulty with assertiveness and communication and would be happy to learn more about it with you.

Once you've finished, put the book and your written work in a handy spot for future reference. As life conflicts come up, resolve to reread pertinent chapters and written exercises and use the information you glean to relate to your life at that moment. As you do this, the concepts will become more a part of you, and your communication skills will grow.

1
My Tongue Hurts

Most people have heard the expression "Bite your tongue!" You're about to blurt out a feeling or state an opinion and somebody says, "Bite your tongue!" In other words, "Whatever it was you were going to say, don't say it!"

Everybody knows how much it hurts *literally* to bite your tongue. But biting your tongue *figuratively* can have just as painful consequences.

Take Ellen, for example. She agreed to let her sister and brother-in-law stay at her home for a week until their new house was ready. One week turned into two. Then two weeks became three weeks and three turned into a month. "It wouldn't have been so bad," Ellen angrily explained, "except for some of their habits. I had just bought new furniture, and they would come in, flop down on the couch, and prop their dirty feet up on my brand-new coffee table! What's more, they never once helped with any of the meals. Instead, my sister would come in and make subtle hints about being hungry until I got up and fixed something. She would just sit in the family room and watch TV."

"Did you try asking them to join in preparing the meals?" someone asked her.

"What? And have them angry with me?" she exclaimed. "You've got to be kidding. I could never do that."

Ellen was extremely angry about her situation. She was so angry that it kept her awake at night, caused her to be irritable with her own family, and made her stomach feel tied in a knot. She found herself praying for the day when her sister and brother-in-law would leave. Ellen was "biting her tongue," all right . . . and it was certainly painful!

Now, biting your tongue isn't always a bad thing to do. There may be times when what you would say impulsively would not help the situation at all. In fact, it might make it worse. But unfortunately many people, like Ellen, see keeping quiet as a rule that cannot be violated under any conditions. For these people, truly unfortunate consequences can result.

Marsha came to counseling reporting that her life was a shambles. She was an active Christian woman and mother of a delightful toddler, but she was sure there was no hope for her marriage. She insisted that her husband, Ron, who was away from home with his job frequently, cared nothing for her, would not communicate with her, and would certainly never agree to come to counseling with her.

As the story unfolded, however, it became apparent that Marsha had not even asked Ron to come to counseling, she was so certain he would refuse. Whenever Marsha and her husband had a conflict, she would just stop talking to him and try to be obedient to whatever he wanted. Sensing that all was not right between them and being frightened by conflict himself, Ron found more and more ways to be away from home, hoping that his absence would make things better. Their marriage was on the brink of disaster not because they argued too much but because they rarely even talked at all.

Fortunately, with training in being more assertive, Marsha began to learn positive ways to communicate her long-standing concerns to Ron. She was startled to find, once she began to express her concerns, that Ron actually listened to her and responded well. In fact, he told her that it was a relief just to know what the problems were instead of constantly pretending they weren't there.

In other words, holding back and not expressing yourself is not necessarily the nice, much less the best, thing to do. Psychologists have long noted that holding back conflictual feelings can lead to both emotional and physical stress. Persons who bite their tongues may find themselves victims of headaches, coronary heart disease, muscle tension, gastrointestinal problems, or a host of other physical problems. Some professionals have estimated that as much as 75 percent of all visits to physicians are made by people suffering from a stress-related problem.[1] And many stress problems are in turn related to unresolved interpersonal conflict.

It would be one thing if the costs of biting one's tongue were limited to the one who keeps quiet. But, as in the case of Marsha and her husband, relationships with others are often hurt in the process. This is perhaps the biggest cost of self-effacement and also the most paradoxical one.

Most people who don't speak up assume that this will help, not hurt, their relationships with others. A husband will not tell his wife his business is failing because he doesn't want to worry her. Sensing that something is wrong, she begins to worry anyway; in fact, she worries more, precisely because she doesn't know what is going on. She sees him spending more time at the office and, lacking information to the contrary, wonders incorrectly if she is no longer attractive to him. Rather than helping, the husband's quietness has hurt their relationship.

The intentions of this husband, and the intentions of most people like him, are good. But good intentions don't necessarily lead to positive outcomes.

For people to understand each other, they have to talk to each other. There has to be communication. They have to be able to speak up. But many people are afraid to do that because they fear it won't work. They have tried at some point in the past to speak up to someone and have had a bad outcome. Here are some of the things that people say go wrong when they speak up:

The other person took what I had to say in the wrong way or took it personally.

The other person got angry, hateful, rude, etc.

I fumbled over my words and didn't say what I really meant to say.

The other person seemed to listen but did nothing.

The other person listened but gave me the cold shoulder later.

The other person made a joke out of what I said.

The other person didn't listen.

I couldn't find a way to say how I felt.

I got angry.

I felt guilty for speaking up and gave up before finishing.

I said something I wished I hadn't.

All these things do sometimes happen when people attempt to communicate with others. But they don't have to happen as much as they do. The key to good communication is to learn how to communicate assertively and to learn the differences between communicating assertively and communicating passively or aggressively—two of the much less effective ways that people use.

The next chapter describes some of these options for relating to others.

2

Powder Kegs, Cream Puffs, and Things in Between

Whenever you set out to learn something new, the first thing you have to do is learn the language that goes with it. When we first began to study psychology, we kept a dictionary of psychological terms close by. The same is true of those who study computers, stamp collecting, or farming. Learning about assertiveness is no different. You have to learn the language.

To learn to be assertive, one must first know what assertiveness is. *Assertiveness is a skill of expressing one's feelings, thoughts, and preferences in ways that take into account one's own rights and feelings and also the rights and feelings of others. It has as its goals clear communication, the equitable resolution of conflicts, and increased intimacy between people.* Let's look at this definition more closely.

1. *Assertiveness is a skill.* A skill is something that you learn. It is not an innate ability. You can learn to be more assertive, and as you do so you can develop and refine that skill. You can practice and become good at it.

2. *Assertiveness is a skill of expressing.* Expressing oneself is a form of behavior. It is an observable activity that people can see and, to some extent, measure or categorize. If you refuse someone by saying no to them, that word "no" is a noticeable behavior that can be measured by the number of times you say it, the intensity in your voice when you speak, and so on. Assertiveness is not some vague concept. We can see when it does or doesn't occur.

3. *Assertiveness is a skill of expressing one's feelings, thoughts, and preferences.* Thoughts include opinions, attitudes, and beliefs. Feelings are emotions like anger, love, joy, sadness, hurt, and concern: human emotions. Preferences may include interests, requests, suggestions, and wants. Note that when you express positive feelings such as love and joy you are being assertive too.

4. *Assertiveness is a skill of expressing in ways that take into account one's own rights and feelings and also the rights and feelings of others.* This is one of the most important aspects of true assertiveness. When I am truly assertive, I assume that I'm important enough to have my own opinions and feelings. But I am also concerned about the person I am behaving assertively with. I assume that this other person has rights and feelings too.

5. *The goals of assertiveness are clear communication, the equitable resolution of conflicts, and increased intimacy between people.* When we communicate clearly, we express ourselves in a way that allows others to make an accurate assessment of what we are trying to say. With clear communication, there is greater consensus that what is being said is what is heard, and that what is heard is what is meant. As we will see later, developing clear communication requires (1) an understanding of how we communicate and (2) practice with the skills needed to communicate.

Another major goal of assertiveness is the equitable resolution of conflicts. Conflicts are unpleasant, but they are an inevitable part of life. In the New Testament, Paul's letters to the early churches often contain advice on resolving church conflicts. As long as there are people with different ideas, there will be the potential for conflict. The key is to learn ways to handle differences as equitably as possible so that each person's concerns are taken into account.

Finally, assertiveness fosters greater intimacy between people. When people feel that they understand clearly and directly what others are saying to them and can speak freely with others, they naturally tend to grow closer. A sense of trust is built. They are willing to relate to each other and work together.

Now you know something about what assertiveness is. It is equally important to know what assertiveness is not.

AGGRESSIVE POWDER KEGS

Assertive people are not "powder-keg people." You've probably met a powder-keg person. You feel as though you're walking on eggshells when you're with such people. Like a real powder keg, they seem ready to explode at any moment.

Aggressive or powder-keg people are often angry, obnoxious, irritable, selfish, and defensive human beings. Like assertive people, they are interested in expressing their personal feelings, thoughts, and preferences. But unlike assertive people, powder-keg people are relatively unconcerned about the rights and feelings of others. In fact, they tend to run roughshod over others' rights in the attainment of their own goals. We term this aggressiveness, not assertiveness.

Often this type of aggressiveness is more than just a behavioral style. It is a way of looking at life. People who behave aggressively tend to see life in a harshly competitive and pessimistic way. They suppose that most people are evil and that, if you don't keep your guard up, others will take advantage of you. A common motto of aggressive people is, "Get them before they get you!" Because of this philosophy, they are often biased in their view of others. They even see people who mean well as potentially harmful to them and assume that another's friendliness is just a cover for manipulation.

Underneath, powder-keg people are not as self-assured as they seem. Most often they have very poor self-images. It is as though they have to compensate for their lack of self-confidence by behaving as forcefully and aggressively as they can.

An old fellow who shot pool used to say tongue-in-cheek to young players, "If you can't shoot good, just shoot hard." He meant that what these players lacked in skill and self-confidence, they might make up for by shooting forcefully and hoping that something would fall in the pocket. This is the strategy of many aggressive powder-keg people: If you lack confidence, mask it by throwing your weight around; make up for it by shooting hard in life.

Aggressive people do seem to get their way a lot . . . but at what cost? Usually at the cost of being severely alienated from others. Most people don't like to be around powder-keg people, and while they may accede to the powder keg's wants over the short term, they are likely to resist them over the long term. As one victim of an aggressive tirade told us recently, "I went along with her this time, but it will be a long time before I do it again."

There is another sad thing about the aggressive life-style. It tends to maintain itself in a vicious cycle.

For example, Al Aggressive sees most other people in a negative light. He behaves toward them in an agitated, defensive way. Eventually, even the people who really care about Al become frustrated with his caustic style and withdraw from him. Al, not recognizing his own part in this cycle, immediately blames the other person. "It just goes to show you," he says. "Those people who say they care are just like everyone else. They aren't there when you need them. You can't trust them." Al then becomes even more sure that the world is filled with nasty people and that "you must get them before they get you!" Little does he realize that many of the people who scowl at him are simply mirroring the scowl that is already imprinted on his own face.

There are two other reasons why aggressiveness tends to maintain itself in a vicious cycle. One is obvious: Whenever Al Aggressive is able to get what he wants, that's a reward for Al even if he had to bully his way into getting it. There's at least some payoff involved, and where there's a payoff it's tempting to do the same thing again. Many people do accede and give in to Al.

The other, not so obvious, fact is that behaving aggressively provides a release of tension . . . at least over the short term. A few years ago, "ventilation" therapies became very popular in counseling. Clients were encouraged to scream and shout at one another, go home and beat their pillows, and let their anger out whenever they felt like it. The theory was that unless the anger was released, or "ventilated," the person would suffer stress, ulcers, and headaches from having too much pent-up anger.

There is some truth to this theory. Giving vent to anger and aggression can lead to an immediate reduction in tension. However, there is a catch. The latest research shows that expressing aggression in this way leads to more, rather than less, need to do so in the future. Furthermore, the tension returns —often very quickly. As researcher Leonard Berkowitz has observed, ventilating aggression breeds more aggression, not less. Thus, rather than reducing tension, frequent release of aggression may actually lead to more, rather than less, tension.[2]

The evidence shows that behaving assertively instead of aggressively can fulfill very adequately the need to reduce the tension we feel when we're angry. In addition, it decreases the need to behave aggressively in the future. Common sense explains why. When people behave assertively, they develop closer relationships with others. People who understand and trust one another are less likely to let conflict situations get to the point where outright aggression is displayed.

Over the long term, aggression is a proven route to disaster in interpersonal relationships. It is not nearly as effective as assertiveness.

SELF-EFFACING CREAM PUFFS

Another style of behaving that differs from assertiveness is self-effacement. Self-effacing or "cream-puff" people rarely speak up. They constantly put others ahead of themselves— much to their own detriment. Friends often refer to them as nice but easily swayed; a doormat, a Caspar Milquetoast, a pushover.

Cream-puff people can't say no. When the doctor strikes your knee with a hammer, it produces the knee-jerk reflex. In a similar way, self-effacing people say yes almost reflexively. It is as though the word "no" is not part of their vocabulary. For example:

Friend: Will you take my kids to school today?

Cream Puff: Yes.

Friend: How about tomorrow?

Cream Puff: Okay.

Friend: You're a great friend. I am really busy. Could I count on you to do it next week?

Cream Puff: I guess so, yes.

Don't assume that cream puffs really *want* to say yes. In fact, when the person wants to say yes there is no problem. But self-effacing people often say yes when they would rather say no. Seconds after saying yes to someone, cream puffs experience that twinge in the pit of their stomachs that tells them they have betrayed themselves.

Why do self-effacing people give in even when they would prefer not to? It's partly because they start early in life with the assumption that other people's thoughts, values, feelings, and rights are more important than their own. Once this assumption becomes established, self-effacing people don't even think of their feelings and opinions . . . until it's too late!

This helps to explain why self-effacing Christians even give in to things that go totally against their moral values. When giving in becomes reflexive, it becomes hard to say no even to things you know are wrong. It becomes so automatic that thought does not enter into it . . . until later on.

A young Christian student we'll call Derek was invited to a party. Once he arrived, he found that several of his classmates were popping pills. He immediately began to feel uncomfortable but decided he shouldn't make a scene. Inevitably, one of his acquaintances passed some pills in his direction and, almost automatically, he took them. Later he felt terribly guilty and wondered how he could have been so gullible.

Most self-effacing individuals, like most aggressive people, lack self-esteem. They have a very low image of themselves and their worth. Because they see themselves as so unworthy, they often believe their rights are insignificant compared to others.

Cream-puff people avoid confrontation like the plague. They tend to rationalize their behavior by telling themselves that life is better when differences are not made public. Since most active people inevitably experience conflict, self-effacing people must constantly avoid the normal challenges of everyday life. By doing this they succeed in bypassing much negative interaction, but they also end up missing out on most of the things that make life interesting.

Dr. Terry Paulson, a friend of ours who works as a management consultant, compares this kind of behavior to the game of baseball. He says that there are two ways to avoid striking out in baseball. One is by going to bat and getting a hit. The other is by staying on the bench and never going to bat at all. Staying on the bench is the surest way of never striking out, but it also means that you'll never experience the joy of getting a hit. Bench sitters are similar to cream puffs. They end up not playing the game.

If you think about Dr. Paulson's example, you can guess what happens to self-effacing people inside. Watching the game from the bench may be fairly interesting for a while. But eventually, just watching everyone else play becomes depressing and boring. Not only that, people who stay on the bench are totally helpless to affect the outcome of the game. Bench sitters have no power.

In the same way, self-effacing people eventually find themselves feeling helpless about their lives. They may develop a fatalistic sense about the possibility of change and say things like "That's the way it is; what can I do?" or "I guess this is just my cross to bear." By contrast, assertive people have faith in the possibility of positive change. They see themselves as significant elements in the game of life.

We've seen how assertiveness differs from aggressiveness and self-effacement. Now let's look at a more subtle form of nonassertiveness.

SUBTLE AGGRESSION: THE BACKSTABBERS

Have you ever felt routinely angry when you were around a particular acquaintance but never knew quite why? Have you ever felt angry about something someone said, but you couldn't figure out exactly what it was that angered you? Perhaps you were dealing with subtle aggression.

Subtle aggression, or backstabbing, is just that. It is a manner of expressing anger, resentment, or aggression in a way that does not clearly reveal those negative feelings to the other person. Two examples illustrate what we're talking about.

EXAMPLE NO. 1

Lucy is a 21-year-old college student. She originally planned to go home to visit her parents and attend her home church on Sunday. However, she has two exams the following week and decides instead to stay at school and study. Here is part of the phone conversation between Lucy and her mother:

Lucy: Mom, I've decided to stay at school this weekend to study for my exams.

Mother (with forlorn voice): Oh, that's all right, dear. I'm sure you have much better things to do with your little college friends than to be with your mother and father. We'll just attend church by ourselves.

EXAMPLE NO. 2

Emmet has been angry with his son, Tommy, for some time because Tommy hasn't been taking out the garbage. Emmet has said little about it, though, hoping that Tommy will shape up on his own. Now Tommy wants his dad to come watch him practice soccer in the evenings. Each evening about four forty-five, Emmet remembers his son's practice but always seems to find something to do at the office that keeps him from getting there on time.

Emmet and Lucy's mother are both expressing aggression in subtle ways. Rather than express her disappointment directly, Lucy's mother tells Lucy that everything is all right and then proceeds to give subtle hints that all is *not* all right. Note the subtle but aggressive way she denigrates Lucy's "little" college friends. Note also the appeal to guilt in the mother's statement that they will attend church alone.

Emmet is definitely angry with his son. But rather than communicate his anger assertively, he simply fails to show up for something that is very important to Tommy.

Much backstabbing is done without malicious intent, but it is harmful nonetheless. Often backstabbers feel angry and resentful but do not know more appropriate ways to express their feelings. In a search for a way to express themselves, they somehow assume that the backhanded way is best.

Subtle aggression is one of the most harmful styles of interacting. People who use it aren't communicating clearly and are often misunderstood by others. The chances are extremely remote, for example, that Tommy will realize that his father's absence from practice has anything to do with the garbage detail. Instead, what will probably occur is an increasing alienation between Emmet and his son. Years later, Tommy may wonder why his father was so uninvolved with him. Subtle aggression leads to resentment and, often, to a lifetime of misunderstanding between people. It is not assertive. It is subtle aggression.

TAKING YOUR OWN ASSERTIVE TEMPERATURE

You may have been trying to decide where you fit among these behavioral styles. The fact is, while we may favor one more than others, most of us tend to use all these styles at one time or another.

As many experts have noted, assertiveness is very situational. You may be assertive with your best friend, self-effacing with your boss, and subtly aggressive with your spouse. The degree of assertiveness varies according to the person you are with, where you are, and a number of other factors.

The primary purpose of this chapter is to help you recognize some basic styles of communication. The hope is that you will then look at your own life for evidence of each of them.

After our workshop discussion of these styles, people often

come up and say things like "That aggressive one sounds just like my husband" or "You really pegged my self-effacing brothers." While we want you to be able to notice these styles in other people, we feel it's most important to notice them in yourself. If that happens, then the purpose of this chapter has been accomplished.

3

A Message from God:
"Speak Up!"

It happens often. I'm talking with a new acquaintance who happens to be a Christian and the conversation turns to assertiveness. "I'm not sure," the person begins, "that being assertive is really proper for a Christian. I mean, aren't we supposed to 'turn the other cheek' and 'go the second mile'? How can you really follow Jesus' example of meekness and also speak up?"

These are real questions and shouldn't be passed over lightly. They are asked by sincere Christians who carefully study the scriptures. However, a serious review of scripture and of assertiveness will reveal that they are based on only a partial view of the evidence.

We've already discussed the fact that assertiveness is not aggressiveness. We've said that assertiveness expresses concern for others as well as for oneself. But didn't Jesus go a step farther? Didn't he model and teach *complete* self-effacement?

The answer is *no!* While Jesus did sacrifice self, this does not account for the diversity of ways in which he responded to others. Much scriptural evidence indicates that Jesus was not only mild and giving but was also confrontative, openly angry, and positively assertive toward others.

Most of us have grown up with some strong stereotypes about what Jesus was like. Unfortunately, many of these are based more on motion pictures and other popular media than they are on the Jesus revealed in the Bible.

Movies have sometimes portrayed Christ as such a quiet,

unassuming man that he appears almost anemic. In the media, Jesus speaks in almost imperceptible whispers and stares at the ground as he talks. Soft music plays in the background.

Fortunately, motion pictures have the advantage of close-up photography and sensitive microphones to record such scenes. However, the real Jesus spoke up! He was not always quiet, unassuming, and deferring.

Let's test our theory. Take a moment to read Mark 3:1–5 below. Pay special attention to Jesus' behavior, words, and feelings.

> Then Jesus went back to the synagogue, where there was a man who had a paralyzed hand. Some people were there who wanted to accuse Jesus of doing wrong; so they watched him closely to see whether he would cure the man on the Sabbath. Jesus said to the man, "Come up here to the front." Then he asked the people, "What does our Law allow us to do on the Sabbath? To help or to harm? To save a man's life or to destroy it?"
>
> But they did not say a thing.
>
> Jesus was angry as he looked around at them, but at the same time he felt sorry for them, because they were so stubborn and wrong. Then he said to the man, "Stretch out your hand." He stretched it out, and it became well again.

Note several things in this account. First, Jesus went to the synagogue of his own volition and healed the man despite the fact that his opponents were obviously watching him. Second, he explained his behavior to his enemies. Finally, the scripture indicates that Jesus' attitude during the incident was a mixture of controlled anger and sadness. Jesus' words, feelings, and behavior were all assertively expressed!

Exercise 1

Take a moment to imagine a modern, self-effacing follower of Jesus, Dorothy Doormat. Think of her in the role of Jesus in the passage. Write a paragraph in your notebook, paraphrasing the verses as you think they would have read if Dorothy Doormat had been in Jesus' place.

Here is one way of interpreting how Dorothy might have handled the situation:

Dorothy tried to avoid going to the synagogue, because she knew there were people there who would try to accuse her. "It's better to avoid conflict than to make waves," she thought. When she finally did arrive, there was a man there with a paralyzed hand. A number of people were watching to see if she would heal him. "Oh, my, why did I ever come here in the first place?" Dorothy worried to herself. "Perhaps the man could come back and be healed tomorrow when the Sabbath is over. After all, what's a day one way or the other? And that would make everybody happy. Maybe if I just stay quiet and keep a low profile, nobody will even notice that I'm here."

What a far cry Dorothy's actions are from those of Jesus! Yet well-meaning Christians sometimes suggest that the Dorothy Doormats in the church are, by far, the most Christlike. As the exercise suggests, nothing could be further from the truth. Dorothy Doormats do not follow the example of Jesus.

Numerous other biblical incidents indicate that Jesus was assertive. In Mark 10:13–15, people brought their children to Jesus, wanting him to touch them. The disciples, thinking this was a waste of time, scolded the people. But Jesus, when he noticed, "was angry and said to his disciples, 'Let the children come to me.' " Jesus assertively stated his position.

Again and again the biblical record provides evidence of Jesus' loving, open, and direct style of communicating. When a rich young man hastily asked Jesus what he needed to do to receive eternal life, Jesus spoke briefly about the commandments and then "looked straight at him with love and said, 'You need only one thing. Go and sell all you have and give the money to the poor, and you will have riches in heaven; then come and follow me' " (Mark 10:21). Notice how love for the man prompted Jesus to speak up assertively.

When the High Priest asked Jesus if he was the Messiah, Jesus didn't respond with long-winded speeches or political double-talk. He simply said, "I am" (Mark 14:62). And in the various accounts of Jesus calling his disciples to follow him (Mark 1:16–20; 2:13–14; Luke 5:1–11), he is both clear and to the point in his requests. Jesus was not bashful when it came to his identity and his need for disciples.

In addition, Jesus allowed himself to care assertively for others. In John 4:1–42, Jesus meets the Samaritan woman at a well. As John points out, Jews would not even use the same dish as a Samaritan. Yet Jesus not only asked the woman to draw him a drink but also talked caringly and knowingly about her needs. He did not stand back because of custom. He boldly ventured out to meet her.

And, though not as frequently, the scriptures suggest that Jesus also cared assertively about his own needs and those of his disciples. This is most clear when Jesus takes time out from his hectic pace for personal rest and prayer (Mark 6:30–32; Luke 9:10–11; 22:39–44). We have known far too many people who, with good intentions, have worked themselves to death, believing all the while that they were following the model of Christ. Effective people know that they must take time for personal rest and renewal if they are to be of benefit to others.

But that still brings us back to our original question. Doesn't Jesus clearly instruct us to "turn the other cheek" and "go the second mile" (Matt. 5:38–47)? Doesn't Jesus say that you are blessed if you are meek (Matt. 5:5)? The answer to these questions is yes. But answering yes doesn't necessarily mean that being assertive is inappropriate. Much has to do with understanding the meaning and intent of the scriptural passages.

The Greek word for the meek in Matthew 5:5 is *praeis.* The word has two origins. Its Hebrew origin suggests humbleness and obedience. Its Greek origin suggests a quality of controlled strength, much like that of a wild animal that has been tamed. William Barclay says that New Testament "meekness" refers to a strong but disciplined self that has come under God's control.[3] The modern world sees the word "meek" and pictures a weak, spineless character. That's much different from what the people of the New Testament had in mind.

Then what is the intent of Jesus' instruction to go the second mile? Read the passage carefully.

You have heard that it was said, "An eye for an eye, and a tooth for a tooth." But now I tell you: do not take revenge on someone who wrongs you. If anyone slaps you on the right cheek, let him slap your left cheek too.

(Matthew 5:38–39)

David Daube has noted that the "eye for an eye" was rarely practiced literally in the time of Christ.[4] Jesus is thus using strong figurative language to make a point. And the point is about revenge (see v. 39), not about the virtues of nonassertiveness. Jesus knew that while his listeners didn't demand an eye for an eye anymore, they were no less vindictive inside. And vindictiveness never leads to harmony, true restitution, or conflict resolution.

A counselor friend of ours tells a story that illustrates a modern application of this truth:

When I was consulting at a general hospital, several physicians asked me to go and counsel with a woman who was "resisting" treatment for a severe infection. When I got to the floor it was obvious that the whole staff was in turmoil. Several of the nurses looked at me in disbelief when I said I was going to try and talk to the woman. "You won't get anywhere with her," one said. I had the feeling that the staff might be placing bets on whether I would come out of the woman's room alive!

When I entered the room, I found a woman lying in bed, smoking a cigarette and angrily looking out the window. "What do you want?" she demanded loudly. Ignoring the provocation in her voice, I reached for a chair, sat down, told her exactly who I was, and then said, "This whole ordeal must be really painful for you." Immediately, the tears began to come and the anger turned to mourning. Yes, it was extremely painful. The infection was painful, the treatments were painful, everything was painful, and nobody seemed to understand. She had family problems and a lot of other concerns that went far beyond the four walls of the hospital room.

Was the counselor assertive? Yes. By avoiding vindictiveness, turning the other cheek, and not taking the woman's anger personally, he was able to express concern for her assertively.

And because he was able to express concern, a relationship was formed and a chance to resolve the conflict over her treatment was begun. Jesus would probably have done the same thing.

We all know what Al Aggressive would have done. He would have told the woman where to get off as soon as she raised her voice. And what about Dorothy Doormat? Dorothy would probably have found numerous ways to keep from going into the room in the first place.

Exercise 2

Pick several chapters out of the Gospels at random. Use one of the newer Bible translations, such as the *Good News Bible.* Read each chapter carefully, paying attention to the words and behavior of Jesus. In each of these chapters, would you consider Jesus' behavior self-effacing? Assertive? How do you think a person like Dorothy Doormat would have handled similar situations? How would you contrast Jesus' behavior with what Al Aggressive might have done?

Recently, a young ministerial student named Jim participated in one of our workshops. He was single and rooming with another young seminarian. When they moved in together, they both agreed that they would share the household duties. Several months had passed, and Jim was the only one doing the dishes. "I know I shouldn't feel resentful about such a little thing," he said apologetically, "but I'm getting so angry, I'm thinking about moving. And this fellow is a good Christian friend in most other ways."

Through the workshop, Jim learned an appropriate way to express his feelings to his roommate and to negotiate a resolution to the dishwashing problem. Though a bit anxious, he then went and actually talked to his roommate. When Jim returned to the workshop the next week, he was ecstatic. To his surprise, he found that when he confronted his roommate in a calm and caring way, his roommate was more than open to solving the problem. What's more, the resolution of one small problem led to such a positive change in their relationship that Jim described the whole situation as a kind of spiritual experience.

Assertiveness is like that. It is a risk of faith. I act assertively, hoping ultimately to create better relationships. Self-effacement is avoidance of risk-taking. It is a "run and hide" philosophy that hopes that things will get better by themselves. It avoids conflict, sometimes to the point of succumbing to things that go totally against one's values. God wants us to speak up, not to hurt others but to be clear with them, not to damage relationships but to further them, not to create more friction but to work through friction to greater intimacy.

4
Talking to Yourself:
The First Step

It's a bright, pleasant day, and you're driving down the highway in the passing lane. As you approach the next car in the slow lane, you happen to notice that the driver is engaged in an animated conversation: holding the wheel with one hand, gesturing with the other, and talking about something obviously of great importance to him. As you come up alongside, you look more closely to catch some clue as to why this conversation is so important, only to realize in amazement that there is no one in the passenger's seat! The man is talking to himself!

An old saying has it that talking to yourself is a sure sign of going crazy. The fact is, however, that all of us talk to ourselves. Of course, most of us are seldom so open about it as the driver going down the highway. But we do it just the same: under our breaths . . . in our heads. And we spend a large part of our days doing it.

When we go to an important business meeting, we rehearse in our minds what we're going to say, what others might say, and how we'll respond. We talk to ourselves silently about all the possible outcomes of the meeting.

When a man asks a woman for a date and is turned down, he may say things to himself like, "What's wrong with me?", "It must have had something to do with my braces," "She's really missing out on a good opportunity," "That's too bad, it could have been fun," or a whole host of other inward messages.

SELF-TALK

Psychologists call these silent messages "cognitions." For our purposes, we can call them "inner thoughts" or "self-talk."

Most of us take these inner thoughts for granted. We don't pay much attention to them, but they have a great deal to do with the way we act. Dr. Albert Ellis, a well-known psychologist, says that being in a particular situation usually triggers certain kinds of inner thoughts, and these thoughts usually determine the type of action a person takes in that situation.[5]

For example, if you tried to start your car to go to work in the morning and it wouldn't start (situation), you might think, "This just proves it's going to be a rotten day" (self-talk), and go crawl back in bed (action resulting from thought).

On the other hand, you might also have thought, "It's irritating that the car won't start, but there are other ways to get to work (self-talk)." Then you might call a friend down the street to ask her to drop you at the bus stop (action).

The situations in these examples are the same, but the actions that follow from each of them are different, largely because of the self-talk that takes place between the start of the problem situation and the action that follows.

SELF-TALK AND ASSERTIVENESS

Inner thoughts also have a great deal to do with whether a person acts assertively or not. Some thoughts are much more conducive to behaving assertively than others.

Suppose, for example, that Linda goes in to see her boss, Mr. B, to ask for a raise. She has carefully evaluated her seniority and work record at the company and feels that she is justified in requesting additional pay. However, on that day when she begins the long trek down the hall to Mr. B's office, something happens. A number of inner thoughts intrude on her all at once. She thinks to herself, "Is this really the right day? I didn't do my best on that new account yesterday. Maybe I should wait.

When George went in to see Mr. B for a raise last week, Mr. B scolded him for his work and refused. What if that happens to me? I certainly don't want to get fired."

It goes without saying that if Linda thinks these thoughts for a very long time, she'll get to Mr. B's office, put her hand on the doorknob, stop, turn around, and go back to her desk. Why? Because of something Mr. B did to her? Not at all. She hasn't even seen him. She doesn't walk through the door because she has just engaged in self-talk about all the reasons why she shouldn't speak up and ask Mr. B for a raise.

Exercise 3

Assume that Linda, in the foregoing example, does deserve a raise. If you look closely, you'll find a number of possible fallacies in her inner thoughts. Write down at least two of them in your notebook.

In analyzing Linda's thoughts, you probably realized that she made some very quick negative inferences without considering any contradictory evidence. For example, while Mr. B may have scolded George last week, it may also be true that George has the worst record in the company. Also, the fact that she made a mistake on an account the day before may or may not have anything to do with whether this is the right day to ask for a raise. And when she tells herself she doesn't want to get fired, she makes the assumption that everything she thought before leads to the conclusion that she probably will be fired if she asks for a raise. If you analyze this inner conversation carefully, there is nothing in it that leads to the conclusion that she will lose her job.

The best way to request a raise assertively is to begin with *honest* self-talk. For example, as Linda begins to walk down the hall toward Mr. B's office, it will be only natural for her to feel her body tense up a bit. After all, it is uncomfortable to ask for a raise. But instead of letting her tension scare her even more, she can use it as a signal to put positive inner thoughts into action. As she notices her tension, she can say to herself, "Hmm, I'm getting keyed up. Asking for a raise is going to be difficult, but I think I can handle it. I'll just take a deep breath and keep moving. Mr. B has a right to turn down my raise request, but I also have a right to ask, as long as I do it in an assertive, caring way. And if I ask in that way, he's much less likely to get angry or to put me down." It's obvious that if Linda thinks like this, she will greatly increase the chance that she'll walk through Mr. B's door, make her request, and do it in a reasonable way.

CREATIVE SELF-TALK

We call this style of thinking "creative self-talk." It can be learned and, once learned, can be applied to a variety of situations in life. However, to learn creative self-talk requires a systematic plan.

Many people aren't very systematic thinkers. When faced with a situation, they go through a hodgepodge of random thoughts, worry, conjecture, and rumination before coming to a decision. Others make decisions without much thought at all. They come to a conclusion based on their mood, intuition, or impulse. Either method is filled with potential difficulty.

Creative self-talk can help you develop thoughts more conducive to behaving assertively. It can also help you develop a more systematic plan for dealing with life situations in general. A look at many successful leaders will show that one reason for their success is their ability to think clearly and systematically before they act.

Helen Keller felt that there are four main things to learn in life: to trust God without hesitation, to behave with the highest motives, to love sincerely, and "to think clearly without hurry or confusion."[6] She was right on all four counts. Let's look at three systematic steps for learning to think clearly and use creative self-talk.

1. LISTEN TO YOUR BODY'S EMOTIONS

Our bodies are very sophisticated pieces of equipment. Aside from all their other functions, they provide us with signals when we are in conflict or stress and even when we are in positive or exhilarating situations. Many of us aren't very sensitive to these body cues, but they are there just the same. You have heard the old sayings: "He's a pain in the neck," "My stomach's tied up in a knot," "She's got cold feet." These aren't just figures of speech. They are real physiological events that happen to people when they are under stress or conflict. Here is a list of some of these processes:

Cold extremities (hands, feet)

Increase in muscle tension (such as in neck, back, face)

Headaches

Gastrointestinal problems

Increased heart rate

Faster respiration

Sweating

Dryness of the eyes and throat

Flushing of the face

The trick is to learn to listen more closely to our bodies when these kinds of physiological changes take place. By teaching ourselves to be consciously aware of these body cues when they happen, we can begin finding ways to deal with them creatively.

An apartment manager we'll call Gwen tended to shy away from tenants who might be angry with her. Through therapy she recognized that in difficult tenant situations her stomach would get tight and her face would turn red. Previously, she had assumed that such physiological reactions meant she was out of control and had better avoid these situations. But now she learned to use these automatic physical responses as cues to put her creative problem-solving abilities to work.

Learning to be sensitive to your body's emotions is like learning to be sensitive to the warning lights in your car. First, you have to know where the warning lights are to pay attention to them. With your body, you have to know your unique warning spots. For some people it's a nervous stomach, for others it's a racing heartbeat.

Next, you have to stop and see when the warning lights go on. If you listen to your body, you allow these warnings to become signals for creative action rather than meaningless frenzy. When a warning light goes on in your car you don't become hysterical. You use the light as a signal to help you consider what you will do next: Slow down? Stop the car? Find a service station? The same is true of your body's signals. You can act creatively once you know what is happening.

Exercise 4

Think back to the last three situations in which you felt strain or stress. List them in your notebook.

In what area(s) of your body did you feel that stress? Make a note of the area(s) alongside each situation you have listed. Do you always experience your emotions physically in the same area(s)?

Your body is your friend, not your enemy. Pay attention to its signals.

2. IDENTIFY NEGATIVE SELF-TALK

Once you learn to assess your body's emotional signals and see them as indications to begin some creative self-talk, you've already taken a giant step toward behaving assertively.

A second major step is to identify your *negative* self-talk. You've already seen some examples of negative self-talk in the way Linda talked herself out of asking Mr. B for a raise.

The varieties of negative self-talk most of us use are many. Perhaps you'll recognize some of the more common negative inner thoughts that follow.

"I can't handle this"

"They'll think badly of me if I speak up"

"Since I'm a Christian, I have no right to say anything"

"Jesus said, 'Love your neighbor as yourself,' and that means I should forget my own needs"

"This situation is terrible, awful, hopeless, impossible, devastating" (pick one)

"I'm certain to fail"

"What can I do?"

"Maybe if I ignore it, it will go away"

"I must not fail at this; I must be perfect, the best, or I will be nothing"

"You can't teach an old dog new tricks"

"They're not going to listen to me anyway"

"I'm no good"

"I don't want to agree, but I guess I will"

"They're terrible"

"I'll get them back for this"

You have probably said some of these things to yourself at one time or another. If you have, you're certainly not alone.

Take the case of Bill, for example. Bill was one of the outstanding young men at Central Church. He was choir director, Boy Scout troop leader, and teacher of a weekly study group in his home. Bill worked as an accountant for a local business. One day, Bill was going into the church office to leave some materials for the choir. There he ran into John Wilson, his associate

minister. The conversation went something like this (Bill's negative inner thoughts are inserted in brackets):

Mr. Wilson: Hi, Bill, you're just the man I wanted to see.

Bill: [Oh, no! I hope he's not going to ask me to take on
something else.] Oh, hi! (grinning) It's nice to see you.

Mr. Wilson: Bill, I'm really impressed with the job you've
been doing with the Boy Scouts, and I've been wondering. We
have some seventh-grade children who are without a Sunday
school teacher . . .

Bill: [Uh-oh, he's going to ask me to teach a class. I'd do it
if I had more time, but I'm not spending enough time with
my own kids as it is. But how can I say no to my pastor?]

Mr. Wilson: . . . and seventh grade is really a crucial time for
these children in their Christian development. I don't think
we could find a better person than you to do the job.

Bill: [What will he think of me as a Christian if I turn down
this opportunity? Didn't Jesus say to go the second mile? I'm
being too concerned about my own rights when I should be
yielding them to others.]

Mr. Wilson: What about it, Bill? Can you take on this special
ministry for us?

Bill: Well, sure. It'll be a little difficult, but I guess I can
handle it. [After all, didn't Jesus teach us to put others first
and ourselves last?]

Mr. Wilson: Great, Bill! I knew you would come through. Let
me get the materials for you.

Bill's inner thoughts caused him to agree quickly to something
he was obviously reluctant to do. You can predict that within a
few months Bill will be depressed or resentful because he added
another responsibility to an already overloaded schedule. He
may get irritable with the seventh-grade children, and he'll surely
feel guilty about not spending more time with his own family. But

then he will quickly cover these feelings with the thought that, as a Christian, agreeing to teach was all he could do. He will not stop to be honest with himself about what he is doing.

That's why it's so important to identify your negative self-talk. By identifying these thoughts and becoming conscious of them, you can deal creatively with them. If you're not conscious of them, you won't be in control of their effects on you. Being aware of them allows you to analyze the truth or falseness of these thoughts and eliminate or modify the ones that make no sense.

3. BEGIN CREATIVE SELF-TALK

This is the key step in the process. At this point you consider the interpersonal situation and begin to formulate rational, reasonable, and realistic inner thoughts. This creative self-talk considers both the pros and cons of the situation, the positive and negative. It is thus very realistic and doesn't gloss over problems.

But it is solution- or creativity-oriented. That is, creative self-talk has as its final purpose solving a problem or making a situation better. It is thinking with a creative purpose. Negative self-talk has no such purpose. In fact, negative self-talk thwarts creative solutions and leads to feelings of hopelessness and depression.

The last section listed some common examples of negative inner thoughts. Let's match them with some alternative creative inner thoughts.

Negative Self-talk	*Creative Self-talk*
"I can't handle this"	"This may be tough, but I'll find a way to handle it"
"They'll think badly of me if I speak up"	"I am valuable as a person because God says so, not because of what others think"

"Since I'm a Christian, I have no right to say anything"

"Being a Christian may or may not mean that I speak up"

"Jesus said, 'Love your neighbor as yourself,' and that means I should forget my own needs"

"Jesus said, 'Love your neighbor as yourself,' and that means I accept my love for myself and use that to help me love others more"

"This situation is terrible, awful, hopeless, impossible, devastating" (pick one)

"This is unfortunate, frustrating, challenging, hard" (pick one)

"I'm certain to fail"

"I'll search for a way to succeed; if I fail I can start again"

"What can I do?"

"I'll experiment and look for things to do"

"Maybe if I ignore it, it will go away"

"I want to deal with this problem soon so it won't continue to fester"

"I mustn't fail at this; I must be perfect, the best, or I will be nothing"

"As a human being, I may make mistakes, but though they aren't pleasant, I can learn from them"

"You can't teach an old dog new tricks"

"I can keep learning new things for as I long as I decide to"

"They're not going to listen to me anyway"

"I'll never know until I try; let's see if I can find a new way that will encourage them to listen"

"I'm no good"

"I'm a child of God, made in his image"

"I don't want to agree, but I guess I will"

"I don't want to do that, but I will do this"

"They're terrible"	"They're human just like me"
"I'll get them back for this"	"I'll just settle down and relax and make my anger work for me, not against me"

For example, here's the way our friend Bill used creative self-talk to help himself deal more honestly and assertively with the associate minister. Remember, Bill's inner thoughts are in brackets.

Mr. Wilson: Hi, Bill, you're just the man I wanted to see.

Bill: [Uh-oh, I wonder if he's going to ask me to take on something else. Wait a minute. Don't get defeated before you start. You can figure out a way to handle this.] Hello, John, how are you?

Mr. Wilson: I'm fine. Bill, I'm really impressed with the job you've been doing with the Boy Scouts, and I've been wondering. We have some seventh-grade children who are without a Sunday school teacher . .

Bill: [He's asking me to teach the class. Should I say yes? I think God would want me to do the best job I can in all the tasks I accept, and I know if I begin this one, I'll start being less effective at the rest.]

Mr. Wilson: . . . and seventh grade is really a crucial time for these children in their Christian development. I don't think we could find a better person than you to do the job.

Bill: [Well, I'm concerned about the children and their Christian development, but I think there are a number of people in the church who have stronger talents in this area than I do. In fact, I know several of the seventh-grade boys, and I don't think I communicate with them as well as with the ninth-graders.]

Mr. Wilson: What about it, Bill? Can you take on this special ministry for us?

Bill: John, if my circumstances were a little different, I might consider it. But I feel as though I wouldn't be working effectively if I took on anything else right now. Why don't you consider putting a notice in the church bulletin about this?

Mr. Wilson: Well, I can see your point. You are shouldering a lot right now. That's a good idea about the note in the bulletin. I'll try it.

In this situation, creative self-talk made the difference. Through it, Bill was able to respond in an assertive yet caring way to his pastor.

Exercise 5

Recall a recent situation in which you could have been more assertive than you were. In your notebook, in tabular form, record the date and time the situation happened (if you remember), the situation, any bodily emotions you felt, and any negative self-talk that hampered you from being assertive. Then, in a column labeled "creative self-talk," list any inner thoughts you could have had that would have helped you be more assertive.

After you have done this, watch for other situations over the next three days in which you could be more assertive. Record the information for those situations in your table. The sample will help you get started.

QUESTIONS PEOPLE ASK
ABOUT CREATIVE SELF-TALK

People often have questions about creative self-talk. Here are answers to three very common ones.

Q: When you say creative self-talk, aren't you really just talking about thinking positively?

A: Not exactly. Often when people speak of positive thinking they mean glossing over the truth or rationalizing, and that's a real mistake. If you're having a severe conflict with your

Self-Talk

Date and Time	Situation	Bodily Emotion	Negative Self-Talk	Creative Self-Talk
Last Monday 5:30 P.M.	Husband has spent every night the past two weeks playing softball with his friends. Says he's going again!	Tension in stomach Anger Tight jaw	I have no right to ask him not to exercise. He'll go into a rage if I ask. I should be more understanding	I have a right to ask; he has a right to say no. If he gets angry, I'll just keep cool. Maybe we can work out a compromise.

spouse and you encourage yourself to start a discussion about
it by telling yourself, "No problem, everything is going to be
just fine," you're not being honest with yourself. Not only
that, you're likely to be greatly disappointed if your spouse
isn't willing to solve the conflict right away. Creative self-talk
honestly admits the difficulty of certain situations but encour-
ages you to look at all sides and hunt for creative solutions.

Q: Is creative self-talk that easy to do?

A: No one said it's easy. It means time, effort, and some
mistakes. But it can be done and is being done, as countless
people will testify. The main thing is to keep working on it
and not give up when mistakes come.

Q: Sometimes situations happen quickly. I think of great
self-talk after the fact, but not during the situation itself.
What can I do?

A: First congratulate yourself for at least having creative
self-talk *after* the situation is over. Then realize that a similar
situation is likely to happen again someday and think about
how you can better use your self-talk in the future. Finally,
if an interpersonal situation is happening too fast, ask for
"time out." For example: If someone asks you to do something and your self-talk says you're unsure about whether to
say yes or no, ask the other person for time to think about the
request. That way you'll give your creative self-talk time to
develop, and you'll be able to return to the situation later and
handle the request appropriately.

In this chapter you have seen the way your inner thoughts help
to determine your assertive behavior. To develop more assertive
behavior, develop more creative self-talk. Three steps are involved: (1) Listen to your body's emotions, (2) identify negative
self-talk, and (3) begin creative self-talk. Creative self-talk is a
way of thinking that honestly considers both the positive and the
negative in a situation and seeks creative, reasonable answers.

5
How to Be Assertive (And Courteous Too!)

Have you ever read a how-to or self-help book only to realize that the book was good at stating problems but poor at telling how to solve them? If you've read a book like that, you know how disappointed you were.

We don't want that to happen to you here, and that's the reason for this chapter and the ones that follow. In this chapter, we're going to learn some very specific ways to behave more assertively.

Whatever you do, don't skip the following chapters or the exercises. To repeat, assertiveness is a communication skill and, like any skill, develops only with practice.

THE I-MESSAGE AND THE YOU-MESSAGE

A fundamental skill in behaving assertively is to learn to use "I-messages" instead of "You-messages" to communicate with other people.[7] The I-message is a means of communication in which persons use the pronoun "I" (rather than "you") to describe their feelings and wishes. The following illustrations will make this difference clear.

EXAMPLE NO. 1

Helen is angry with her teenage son, Jeff, because the gas gauge registered almost empty after he used the car. She felt he should have bought some gas before bringing the car home.

Helen: Jeff, do you care about this family?

Jeff: Sure, Mom.

Helen: Well, why can't you at least fill the car up with gas after you run all over the countryside?

Jeff: I don't know. I guess I forgot.

Helen: You forgot. It seems as though you forget a lot these days. You've got to learn some responsibility, Jeff.

Jeff: Yeah. . . . Well, why don't you get responsible by mending my trousers? You said you would three weeks ago.

You can see the direction this conversation is going. Notice the number of times the word "you" is used. Underline them and count them. Also notice the *way* in which the word is used. In this context, "you" means "blame." "You" is like pointing the finger in someone's face and accusing him or her of doing wrong.

In saying "you," Helen mistakenly supposes that she will convince Jeff of his wrong, encourage him to apologize to her, and motivate him to put gas in the car next time. Not only is she mistaken, she will also be frustrated. Jeff will not only fail to apologize, he'll also try to strike back at her. That's because You-messages are inherently antagonistic and irritating. They invite fighting and antagonism rather than creative solutions.

Also notice several other poor communication strategies that arise when You-messages are used. Helen uses *questions* at the beginning of the discussion. Questions, especially when used in conjunction with You-messages, have a devastating effect on creative communication. They tend to initiate a combative situation even when one isn't necessary. In this situation, Helen becomes something like an interrogating district attorney and Jeff becomes the witness on the stand. Little resolution is likely under such circumstances.

Notice also that Helen uses *absolute statements* to refer to Jeff's behavior. She implies that he doesn't care about the family, that he runs all over the countryside, and that he forgets a lot. Other common absolute statements are "You never" and "You always." Absolute statements encourage defensiveness from the other person. An old saying applies here: "Nothing is always, never say never." People resent being overwhelmed by absolutes. Helen should stick to the gas-tank problem and not generalize to *all* Jeff's behavior.

Analysis is another poor strategy that comes with You-messages. In analysis you explain another person's behavior *for* them. How many times have you heard people say:

"Your problem is that you are basically insecure and don't stand up to people."

"You don't mean what you said; you're just tired."

"You're a lazy person and that's why you can't accomplish anything."

"You forgot to do your job and now you're blaming me for not reminding you."

If you are like most people, you resent being analyzed even when there's some truth to it. When we're analyzed we feel boxed in. Someone else is deciding about our motives and our feelings without asking us.

In her conflict with Jeff, Helen analyzes. She asks Jeff if he cares about the family. She implies that he doesn't and that not getting gas for the car proves it.

Lecturing is another negative by-product of the You-message. Lecturing in one-to-one personal relationships makes the one being lectured feel one-down, demeaned, and defensive. When Helen tells Jeff he's got to learn responsibility, she's giving him a mini-lecture. Fortunately, she doesn't keep it up. Most people who fall into this communication trap lecture on and on. They alienate the listener before they finally stop. The effect of their message is lost. If Helen had continued, Jeff would have probably turned her off: hummed to himself or put his mind on something else. He would stand there and look as if he were listening, but his mind would be far away.

EXAMPLE NO. 2

Helen might have changed the whole tone of the conversation if she had used I-messages rather than You-messages.

Helen: Jeff, when I go out to the car in the morning and there's no gas in it, I get angry. I also worry that I won't get to work on time. Next time you take out the car, I'd like you to make sure it has at least half a tank of gas in it before you bring it home.

Jeff: Well, you don't always get it filled up either, you know?

Helen: That's true, and I'll watch that, but I'd also like you to agree that when you take the car out, you'll put gas in it if the tank is low.

Jeff: Okay, Mom. You got it.

Helen: Thanks! I appreciate that.

Notice what Helen is doing here. She has radically increased the use of the pronoun "I." Go back and underline the "I"s. Count them.

When *I* go out to the car

I get angry

I also worry

I won't get to work

I'd like you to make sure

I'll watch that

I'd also like

I appreciate that

Her focus is on her own thoughts, feelings, and preferences. And that's where it should be if Helen wants to be assertive rather than aggressive. Helen is the one who is concerned about having gas in the car; she admits that it is her concern. She does not focus on what Jeff's concern should be, nor does she scold him. Rather, she focuses on the fact that the situation is making her life very difficult and she would like to see things changed. You will have to admit that I-messages increase the chances that Helen's car will have gas in it the next time she wants to use it.

THE PARTS OF AN I-MESSAGE

There are three steps in an I-message. These aren't hard-and-fast rules, as we'll see later. But for the sake of learning now, remember these steps:

When (a particular situation or thing occurs)

I feel (state the emotion you feel)

I'd like (state what you'd like to see done or offer to negotiate)

Exercise 6

Read the three steps again. Look back at Helen's I-message dialogue with Jeff and note the three parts in her message. Acting as if you are Helen, write them in your notebook in order: (1) *When* _____, (2) *I feel* _____; (3) *I'd like* _____.
The answers are in Appendix A.

Let's look more closely at each of the three parts to learn specifically what makes them effective.

1. *When:* In this step you're trying to state the problem as clearly and as concisely as possible. In doing this you want to focus as much as possible on the problem itself, not on the other person's motivations or intentions. If you do this, you'll be more likely to stay problem-centered and less likely to engage in You-messages, blaming, or character assassination. When you stay problem-centered and not person-centered, you're more likely to solve the problem.

One helpful way to keep this in mind is to imagine two people

seated opposite each other with a "problem" on the table between them. As long as they look straight ahead and focus on
each other, they compete with each other as to who is right or
wrong and lose sight of the problem. If they look down and
focus on the problem—not on each other—the problem gets
solved!

Nowhere is the issue of problem focus better illustrated than
in marriage. In a troubled marriage the couple constantly focus
on each other rather than on the problem to be solved. For
example, Thad asks his wife, Julie, to clean up a room she's been
promising to clean for weeks. Julie retorts with a list of things
that are wrong with Thad: "You didn't take out the garbage,"
"You're always nagging me," "Your mother didn't teach you
to be very tidy, either." This blaming could go on and on. Before
long, Thad and Julie will totally lose sight of the problem (clean-
ing the room) and be engulfed by the angry pain of insults and
injury. As psychologists, we never cease to be amazed at the
number of couples who come to marriage counseling after a
bitter fight but can't even remember what the basic issue was
that started the conflict!

Successful married couples work together. They focus on the
problem, not on each other. They put the problem "on the
table" between them and encourage each other to solve it. They
realize what members of a good football team know. The primary adversary must be on the other side of the line, not in your
own huddle. While mistakes may be made on your side, they are
resolved for the purpose of solving the problem of getting past
the other team to the goal line. Imagine a football team that
focused only on each other. They'd be so busy fighting, they'd
never get out of the huddle.

Thus, when describing the problem situation, it's important
to stay focused on the problem. Be as concise and to the point
as possible. Simply state the problem situation. Avoid question-
ing, blaming, or analyzing. Stay problem-focused, despite how
negative the other person's immediate responses may be.

2. *I feel:* In the second step of the I-message, you are describing the emotion that you experienced in the problem situation.

This is the difficult step for most people. That's not because most people are unemotional, but because many people have poor skills at identifying what their emotion is at any given moment.

A classic comedy routine we've all seen is the man, obviously furious about something, whose friend calmly asks what he's angry about. In a bellow, the man yells back, "I'm not angry!" As a society, most of us have not learned to identify our feelings accurately, especially negative ones like anger. As we grow up, we're often taught to deny our more negative feelings. In an attempt to keep us from wallowing in negative emotions like anger or self-pity, well-meaning parents and caregivers may attempt to stifle the expression of these emotions altogether. Unfortunately, denying them doesn't make them go away, it just makes us unable to recognize exactly what it is we're feeling.

Another reason we have trouble labeling our feelings is that telling others what we feel is a risk. It's an expression of vulnerability. When I tell you that I love you, or that I'm angry with you, I allow you into my inner world. I do that not only to communicate accurately with you but so that you will know me better. When I do that, I trust that you will not trample on my feelings, but that you will use what I share with you to understand me better and to join me in working out our differences.

The risk involved is that you will not come closer to me. You may ridicule my feelings, you may discount them as unimportant, or you may exaggerate them to such a point that you label me as weird for having them.

In any case, expressing my feelings to you is the only way I can get to know you and you can get to know me. If that is accomplished, we will have the most fertile ground possible for resolving any conflicts that arise.

Exercise 7

How familiar with "feeling words" are you?

Feelings start with either "pleasure" or "pain." All other feelings are spin-offs from these two. In your notebook on a sheet of paper write the phrase *I feel* and then complete the phrase with as many terms for feelings you have had that you can think of. Two examples might be *I feel angry* or *I feel overjoyed.* Compare your list with the one in Appendix B, but don't consider our list exhaustive by any means. You may have experienced feelings that are not on the list.

Expressing feelings is so difficult for some people that they may incorporate the phrase *I feel* into their assertive communication but not actually finish the phrase with a feeling expression. For example, Heather was irritated with her brother Bob for not coming to visit her when he said he would. She could have made a feeling statement to Bob along the lines of *I feel irritated with you.* Instead, she said, *I feel like you don't want to come see me.*

You can see what Heather did. This isn't really an I-feel statement at all. It was a blaming You-message with the words *I feel* tacked on the beginning. Watch out for this in your own conversation. It's easy to do what Heather did, especially if you are hesitant to express what you feel.

3. *I'd like:* In this final step you're making an initial attempt to resolve the conflict by suggesting a change for the better. The I'd-like statement may be a specific request for change ("I'd like you to clean up your room right away"), or it could be an invitation to discuss ("I'd like to sit down and work out our disagreement over this contract as soon as possible").

Sometimes people shy away from including this last step. They may suppose that the first two steps are more important anyway. In fact, the last step is very important because it prevents two things from happening that often ruin an otherwise good assertive message.

First, saying what you'd like to have happen forces you to spend a portion of your communication being constructive. This will prevent your assertive message from degenerating into a complaint or a gripe. In telling what you'd like done in a positive way you're offering creative solutions, or at least you're offering to sit down and work out a creative solution with the other person. Completing your message in a positive way tends to create a positive set for the interchange that follows. It will encourage the other person to be positive with you.

Telling what you'd like is also important because it forces you to *tell* what *you'd* like. Sometimes people come back after trying this three-step formula and say, "It didn't work. That guy didn't listen to my suggestions at all."

"Did you use all three steps?" we ask.

"Yes . . . well, I think I did."

"Exactly what suggestions or requests did you make in the I'd-like part of your message?" we ask.

"Uh—well, I guess I didn't exactly make any. But he should have known what I wanted."

Hoping that the other person will guess what you want is a poor strategy. At best, using this strategy will leave you frustrated and angry most of the time.

Obviously you don't always know what you want, nor do you necessarily want to present a unilateral resolution to the problems. With real conflict issues you'll often want to sit down with the other person, offer your suggestions, listen to the response, and together make up a solution with the greatest benefit for all.

Exercise 8

Recall two conflict situations you had with someone else. Divide your paper in half vertically and, in the left column, write down what you remember saying to that other person. Try to be honest. Then, in the right column, rephrase what you said into a three-part I-message you could have used. Repeat the same process for the second situation.

You may find lots of You-messages in the left-hand "What I Said" column. Or you may find that you have very little to write in the first column because you actually said very little. Either way, translating your communication into an I-message will help you determine a more effective way to say what you wanted to say.

QUESTIONS AND ANSWERS

Q: I've been trying to use these I-messages you talk about. But it seems so unnatural to talk that way. I feel as though it's not me talking, that I'm just playacting. What's the problem?

A: What you're describing is entirely normal. Setting out to drop one habit and start another always feels unnatural at first. When a longtime smoker stops smoking, it feels strange initially. But no one would suggest that just because it feels unnatural to abstain, he or she should begin smoking again. Two things will occur when you *continue* to practice your I-messages despite the awkwardness you feel. First, I-messages will begin to feel more and more natural. Second, you'll begin to adjust I-messages to your own particular personality style and social situation. You'll be less confined to the formula (When—I feel—I'd like) and more able to communicate these basic ideas in a way that fits you.

Q: In other words, you're saying that the When—I feel—I'd like formula isn't the only formula for communicating an I-message.

A: That's right. It's an excellent formula to help you learn how to present I-messages at first. However, as you become more proficient you will discover more latitude in adapting the formula to the unique types of situations you find yourself in. A beginning photographer or artist starts with certain rules of posing or composition and follows them precisely. However, with time and practice one learns to adapt the rules to one's particular needs. Learning to use I-messages works the same way.

Q: I-messages sound nice on paper, but they probably won't work with my husband (wife). He (she) never listens to anything I say.

A: We don't guarantee that I-messages or any other assertiveness skill will be effective with everyone. We do believe that

I-messages increase the probability that you will be able to work through conflicts more positively. In fact, we are constantly amazed at the many spouses who do respond positively to I-messages even after years of marital conflict.

Q: Your I-messages look fine for use in conflict situations, but I thought you said assertiveness helps you in other kinds of situations too. Did you mean that?

A: Yes. I-messages, especially using the When—I feel—I'd like formula, are designed primarily for conflict situations, but they are helpful in many other kinds of situations too. In the next chapter, we'll look at ways to communicate assertively in other types of life events.

6

Assertiveness in Everyday Life

In the last chapter, we learned about I-messages and how they can make a real difference in communication. We saw how using an I-message can help you be honest, direct, and concise and yet still be courteous and loving in conflict situations.

In this chapter we're going to look at how to be assertive in a variety of other life situations. We'll adapt aspects of the I-message for use in some of these situations. In others, we'll describe other helpful tips for communicating effectively.

Again, remember that doing the exercises is very important. You won't become assertive by allowing the thoughts in this book to seep in and change your attitude. Only by taking the action described in the exercises will you change your behavior.

The six types of life situations we deal with in this chapter are the ones most people say they have trouble with. We know our list doesn't exhaust the possibilities, but it does cover some major areas and should give you ideas for the kinds of situations you face.

MAKING REQUESTS OF OTHERS

Making requests of others is a fundamental fact of life. There is no way to go through life without asking for things. Requests may be overt or covert, subtle or clear. When you ask your husband to be home by a certain hour you are, of course, making a request. But you may also be making requests when you go to buy your groceries. You may implicitly be asking for good service, well-marked aisles, and fast check-out lanes. You may also be making an implicit request when you berate friends or family members—or when you give them the cold shoulder.

Requests should be clear. Making clear requests is an important part of letting other people in your life know your likes and dislikes, your wants, preferences, and concerns.

"I'd like to leave on vacation on the thirteenth and return on the twentieth. How does that sound to you?"

"My car broke down. Would you mind dropping some library books off for me when you go downtown tomorrow?"

"I'd like to go out to eat tonight. I don't care where we go. I'd just prefer not to stay home. What would you like?"

"I want you to stop making suggestive comments and jokes!"

You will note that good requests often include the "I'd like" element of I-messages. Good requests sometimes include some statement about how strong the request is: whether it is a mild preference, a wish, or a strong request. Qualifying your request in this way helps the other person respond accurately to what you are asking for. Other people aren't always good at perceiving the seriousness of your request unless you tell them. For example, people who are used to having others make harsh demands may not take your request seriously. Telling them how strongly you want what you want may help them respond to you in an appropriate way.

Another important feature of a good request is that it be concise and direct. Many people attempt to pad their requests with lots of extra words designed to soften the request. Sammi wants a long-ago-borrowed book back from Charlotte. Can you find her request?

Sammi: Oh, by the way, you know that book I think you borrowed from me? It had something to do with the history of civilization. Are you finished with it yet?

Charlotte: Oh, just about.

Sammi: Well, no hurry or anything, but maybe when you get through with it, and you happen to think of it when you're going out, you could drop it by.

Charlotte: Okay, sure.

All this extra verbiage does is hide from Charlotte how serious Sammi is about getting her book back. A much better, yet still pleasant, way for Sammi to ask would be this:

Sammi: By the way, that book on the history of civilization I loaned you; I'd like to get it back by this weekend. Could you return it by then?

Charlotte: Sure, I can bring it by on Saturday afternoon when I go to the store.

Sammi: Great! I'll have some tea for you.

This is concise, direct, yet pleasant and positive. You can see how these features blend to make Sammi's second request clearer and more effective than the first.

On paper, good concise requests look simple, but many people avoid making requests and, when they do make them, do so in subtle, covert ways.

Why do people avoid making direct requests? Usually there is negative self-talk involved. This self-talk can take a variety of forms. For some there is an inner belief that making requests is a selfish means of imposing on others. They avoid asking for things because they don't want others to see them as selfish, rude, or domineering. What they don't understand is that a simple request is rarely viewed as overbearing unless the person making the request is overbearing in manner: that is, aggressive.

For some, the difficulty in making requests has to do with thinking that others ought to know what they want.

"Why should I ask him to help out with the laundry? He ought to know that it needs doing."

"She ought to know better than to be rude. Why should I ask her to be civil with me?"

The fact is, most people aren't very good mind readers and don't realize the impact their behavior has on others. Often, things that seem obvious to us may not be to someone else. Doing the laundry is almost a reflex action for some people but may not be for others. If people are to be clear about what you want, you'll have to tell them. To do otherwise is to assume that others are endowed with powers of perception they simply don't have.

Other people don't make requests because, in the words of one country gentleman, they "don't want to be beholden to nobody." These people believe that to ask anyone for anything is to place yourself in that person's debt, and this is seen as some kind of sin against the spirit of individualism. Most people we've known who try to live this way are lonely people who don't seem to realize that the only way to live happily with others is to live in community with them. The give-and-take of human relationships is part of the essence of friendship and closeness.

An overriding thought that keeps most people from making requests is the idea that they have no right to ask. They put it in down-to-earth ways like this:

"I can't ask her to give me a ride; I've never given her one."

"Who am I to ask him for a favor?"

How much more positive it is to say, "I have a right to ask; they have a right to say no." This is the essence of assertive requesting at the self-talk level. Thinking this thought reminds me that I have the freedom, and sometimes the responsibility, to ask for things. I also can realize that others have every freedom to turn me down.

One final note on making requests. There is a type of request that many people forget about but which is extremely important in life. This is the request for feedback. The request for feedback is a means of asking someone else for an evaluation of how you are doing. Over the past several years, we have made it a practice to ask work supervisors to give us feedback on our performance at regular intervals. This does several things that are ultimately of benefit both to us and to our supervisors. It gives us some indication of what we are doing well and where we need improvement. It lets us be in greater control of our feelings when we get negative feedback: that is, we can ask for the feedback when we're in a mood to take it. It lets supervisors know we are interested in our work and their opinions. Finally, it helps us keep the communication clear and assertive between our supervisors and ourselves. After all, supervisors can also be nonassertive, and they sometimes put off telling us things that might seem negative. Requesting feedback invites a supervisor to be honest and assertive with us. Obviously, asking for feedback can be helpful in many other types of relationships also. It is essential to developing a strong marriage, family, and church.

Exercise 9

Do you have difficulty making requests? If you do, you probably have trouble with certain people and situations.

In your notebook, list five people of whom you have difficulty making requests. Then list five situations in which you have this difficulty.

Now go back and rate each of these items *a, b,* or *c,* according to how difficult they are for you, in ascending order, as follows: *(a)* It would be *slightly* difficult for me to be assertive with this person or situation; *(b)* It would be *moderately* difficult for me to be assertive with this person or situation; or *(c)* It would be *very* difficult for me to be assertive with this person or situation.

Place the appropriate code letter in the margin to the left of the item. Be sure to do this! We will return to these ratings in the next chapter.

REFUSING OTHERS (AND SAYING YES)

Like making a request, saying no seems relatively easy. After all, it's a simple two-letter word. But some people will do almost anything to avoid saying it.

Teresa came for counseling very distraught. She was due to marry a young man in two months. The trouble was, she knew she didn't really want to marry him. In fact, she admitted that she had never wanted to marry him. But somehow she found herself saying yes to every proposal he made to her, from the first date right up to now, almost at the altar. "I know I should have said no to him at the beginning, but he was nice and considerate and I didn't want to hurt him," she explained. "But now, the longer this goes on the harder it gets to tell him no, and the more trapped I feel."

Again, negative self-talk is often involved in preventing a person like Teresa from saying no. Some people don't believe they have the right to turn anyone else down for anything. They fear that others will dislike them or that they will hurt somebody's feelings, so they stifle their own ability to refuse.

Exercise 10

During the next week, watch how seldom people actually use the word no when refusing your requests. Instead, notice how often they beat around the bush or make excuses. While it is often polite to give a simple explanation when you refuse someone, it doesn't help if your explanation confuses the other person or hides the real reason for your refusal.

Some Christians mistakenly believe that being a Christian and being agreeable always go hand-in-hand. For them, giving in is a Christian virtue. A bit of thought will reveal the error in such a belief. Certainly these same people wouldn't suggest that Christian people should give in when matters of Christian ethics or values are at stake.

Even saying yes to those in need isn't always the best thing to do for them. Jill is constantly in financial difficulty. She's known in the family for her fiscal irresponsibility. Usually when Jill gets in a financial bind, she comes to her cousin Doris for a loan. Doris always gives her the money, even though Jill seldom repays the debt. Doris rationalizes her behavior by telling herself that as a Christian she should give to others in need with no thought of return. This might be true if Jill were really in need. But Doris is actually reinforcing Jill's financial irresponsibility rather than helping her get out of her financial problems once and for all. Doris is unconsciously encouraging Jill to see her as a quick source of money. Why should Jill learn to manage her funds when she has her cousin's money available to her? Saying no to Jill *and* offering to help her work out a personal financial plan would be a much more loving and assertive thing for Doris to do.

Being unable to say no also puts the Christian in the position of using talents and abilities unwisely. "Yes" people constantly find themselves doing things that don't make the best use of their time. They often find themselves burning out from the strain of trying to fulfill all the commitments they have made. Jesus recognized this. He didn't agree to everything. Sometimes he took time out for meditation and prayer despite the fact that obvious needs were all around him. When an official came to him and asked him to walk twenty miles to heal the official's son, Jesus didn't go with the man (John 4:46–53). Instead, he simply told the man that when he returned he would find his son well.

As being able to say no is important, so is being able to say yes. Saying yes is often the self-effacing response, but it can also be the response by which we accept a challenge to stretch ourselves, to be more than we have been. Sometimes we say yes to a challenge at work, church, or home, not out of personal preference but as a way of helping ourselves grow.

Dale was very shy. He had great difficulty meeting people and went to social gatherings only because he was too weak to say no. After the first session of assertiveness training, Dale said he was glad the seminar would include training in refusal. "I want to be able to say no to these people who ask me to come to their get-togethers."

Dale had missed the point. In his case, to say no to social gatherings was actually to avoid the possibility of becoming more assertive. Saying yes was an acceptance of the challenge to communicate more effectively with others.

Sometimes the most difficult problem is being able to decide between refusing or agreeing to a request. A great number of the difficult requests we respond to have both positive and negative sides to them. Deciding isn't easy.

As we mentioned before, it's important to give yourself time to think. If someone is pressuring you for a decision, be assertive and tell the person that you haven't decided yet. There's no crime in having ambivalent feelings about a request. The problem arises when a person tries to decide too quickly whether to say yes or no and then is disappointed later with the decision.

Your goal is to "say only 'Yes' when you mean yes, and 'No' when you mean no" (Jas. 5:12). When you give yourself the chance to think things through, you are much more likely to feel comfortable with the decision you make and able to accept the consequences if your decision turns out to be wrong.

Exercise 11

Perhaps there are some situations in which you want to learn to say no more effectively. If so, list them in your notebook.

Being able to say yes can also be an assertive response when it means yes to growth, challenge, and the betterment of all concerned. Think carefully. Are there some situations you'd like to say yes to that you haven't? List them.

Now rate each item in increasing order of difficulty *(a, b,* or *c)* just as you did in the section on making requests. Remember, we'll return to these ratings later.

GIVING AND ACCEPTING COMPLIMENTS

Ask any truly effective manager, parent, teacher, minister, or coach, and he or she will tell you that giving people compliments is one of the most important communication skills in life. There's no doubt that giving compliments or positive feedback is a motivator. But it also brings people closer together. Think of the people who are closest to you. One thing that makes those relationships so positive are the words of support and encouragement that are given back and forth.

This has been called the age of cynicism, an age of criticizing, satirizing, and backbiting. We see it in the news, in comedy, and even in the church and pulpit. We're a society that's good at complaining but not very good at applauding when things go well.

We talk a great deal about constructive criticism but wonder why it seldom works. What we fail to understand is that compliments, when assertive, are some of the most effective teachers we have.

A family came to therapy with a teenage daughter. Two things became apparent as they talked. The girl was very talented and had many fine qualities. She made good grades and was active in church and community activities. However, throughout the session her mother blitzed her with complaint after complaint about all her real and potential shortcomings. After a time, the rest of the family was asked to step out and the daughter remained behind with the counselor. As soon as the door was closed, she broke down completely. "If I only knew what she wants from me," she sobbed. "If she'd just once tell me that I did something right. Then I would at least know I was on the right track."

The girl was right. The beauty of compliments is not just that they help us feel good, it's that when they're presented well, they give us feedback about our behavior. They tell us we're "on the right track."

To do that, a good compliment must be specific. Let's suppose your new secretary does an excellent job of typing a report for you. The margins are correct, there are no misspellings, and she asked you about a questionable item on the original copy rather than simply guessing at it. If you pass by her desk and say something like, "Hey, you're really doing a great job here," you're not giving her specific feedback. On the other hand, you could walk up with the report and say something like this: "I really like the job you did on this report. The margins are just right, there are no misspellings, and I really liked the way you checked on the phrase that was illegible on my copy." This compliment is powerful because it expresses both general support and clear feedback. It helps the new secretary know the exact manner in which she's meeting your expectations.

Here are some more good compliments:

"That was a fine sermon. I especially liked the part about dealing with loss. I lost my brother to cancer, and your words really hit home."

To a young toddler, smiling: "I really like it when you hold your juice cup with both hands" (illustrate with hand motions).

Spouse to partner: "I really get excited when you kiss me on the neck like that."

Exercise 12

In your notebook, list three people that you'd like to give compliments to. Then, briefly but specifically, list the compliments you'd give them. Rate each item according to difficulty (*a, b,* or *c*) just as you did in the last exercise.

The other side of giving compliments is receiving them. Often when people are complimented, they respond with something like "Oh, it was nothing" or "But I didn't do so well later" or something similar. We call this "discounting the compliment," and it's not an assertive response. Not only that, if it goes on long enough, it discourages others from giving you appropriate compliments at all.

One of the best responses of all to a compliment is "Thank you" or "Thank you, I really appreciate that." If unsure about what the compliment is for, it's good to ask for clarification: "What was it that you especially liked about the report I typed?" Responding to compliments with a simple word of appreciation and possibly a request for clarification won't make a braggart out of you. That's what many nonassertive people fear will happen if they genuinely accept a compliment. Saying thank you is a far cry from making such bragging, overgeneralized comments as "I always do an excellent job of things like that" or "Yeah, you're lucky you hired me."

Exercise 13

Watch how you respond to any compliments you receive in the next three days. Record your response on the left-hand side of your paper. If you think you could have made a more assertive response, write down what you could have said on the other side.

From now on, consciously watch for times when others give you compliments and try to respond in more positive ways.

EXPRESSING FEELINGS

In the last chapter, we saw that expressing how we feel can be an important part of I-messages. We also saw that expressing feelings is both a way of letting others know us and a way of knowing others at a deep, personal level. In this section, we look more closely at expressing both positive and negative feelings.

Everybody has feelings. What varies from person to person is the degree to which they express their feelings to others. Most people tend to be *under*expressive of their feelings. They avoid letting others know when they're angry, glad, frustrated, or sad. People who are extremely underexpressive are usually seen by others as overcontrolled, aloof, and unfeeling. They are like the young intellectual we'll call Edward. At first glance, talking to Edward was like talking to a computer. There was no glimmer of energy, happiness, sadness—or anything. Edward talked about everything in a detached monotone. He seemed unaffected by feelings. The truth was that Edward had lots of feelings but had decided that his life would be a lot safer if he could somehow program these feelings out of his life.

Then there are people who don't express feelings because their feeling-word vocabulary is limited. They tend to mislabel their feelings by using one word to refer to several different types

of emotions. Many people go to the doctor and complain of
feeling "nervous," for example. However, for some people nervous means anxious, for others it means depressed, while for still
others it can mean psychotic or severely disturbed. Some people,
fearing words like "anger," will use the words "frustrated" or
"disappointed" when they really mean something stronger. Mis-
labeling feelings can cause others to grossly misunderstand what
you mean and set chains of miscommunication in motion. The
other danger in overusing one feeling word is that after a while
people will tend to ignore you when they hear it. As the husband
of one wife who said she felt slighted exclaimed, "So what?
Everything that doesn't go her way, she says she feels slighted."

There are some people who *over*express their feelings. When
they do this to the extreme, people refer to them as "wearing
their heart on their sleeve." Bolstered by a little pop psychology
or something else, these people let everyone know how they feel
no matter what the circumstances. At one extreme, they seem
to feel a duty to express warm feelings toward everyone. At the
other extreme, they must make sure that everyone with whom
they are angry knows it. It's not appropriate to express every
feeling you have without reservation. There are some situations
where it is important to control what you express about your
feelings.

When people think of expressing feelings assertively, they
usually think of negative feelings (such as anger, disgust, resentment, or frustration). It's also true that positive feelings (e.g.,
love, liking, joy) need to be expressed assertively. Men in our
culture tend to have difficulty expressing positive feelings assertively. When their wives complain that they never say "I love
you," these men reply with things like "I come home, don't I?"
or "I'm a good provider, aren't I?" Sharing your positive liking,
affection, or satisfaction with someone is extremely assertive.

Exercise 14

Look at the feeling words in Appendix B. Adding some of
these words to your vocabulary can make a difference in your

assertive expression. Get some small index cards and copy some of the less familiar words on the cards. Each day put a different card in your wallet or purse or somewhere else where you will notice it. Soon you'll find yourself becoming more accurate in expressing your feelings to others.

Sometimes it's important to restate the strength of your feelings, especially when it's apparent from the conversation that the other person did not understand your feeling expression as you intended. For some people, the word "angry" means hatred, while for others it means slightly irritated. For some people love means a deep and abiding relationship, while for others it means nothing more than a quick opportunity for some affection.

Knowing when to express a feeling is especially important when dealing with very insecure people. It might be a mistake to go in and tell a very defensive, uptight boss that you are angry with him. It could hurt more than it helps to tell your already guilt-ridden mother how much you hate the way she raised you. Knowing when, when not, and how much to express feelings is a talent of discernment that develops with time and practice.

Obviously, it helps to consider who is at the other end of your potential feeling expression. Can the person take it or not? What's your track record and that of others in trying to communicate feelings to this person? Sometimes you will decide that delivering an I-message without the I-feel step is your best alternative.

Expressing feelings assertively requires a good knowledge of feeling words, an ability to specify to others how strong your feeling is, and the good judgment to know when and when not to express feelings. All are important.

Exercise 15

Are there some situations you face in which you think it would be appropriate and potentially helpful for you to express your positive or negative feelings more clearly? List all the ones you can think of in your notebook.

How difficult would it be for you to express yourself assertively in each of these situations? Rate each situation according to difficulty *(a, b,* or *c)* just as you have done before.

LISTENING AND UNDERSTANDING
OTHERS' FEELINGS

We hope by this time we've dispelled any notions you have
that assertiveness is synonymous with selfishness. Assertive people are concerned about their own needs but they're also concerned about others' needs as well. Nowhere is this more evident
than when it comes to assertive listening. Truly listening to
someone else is an act of Christian charity, an act of love.

Too often, people don't listen even when they seem to. To
listen to you fully, I must be able to consider what it might be
like to be in your shoes. Of course, I can't get so caught up that
I flounder in your concerns. Then I can't be of any help. But I
can learn to get past my own biases and preconceptions to sense
how the world looks from your vantage point.

Dr. Carl Rogers, the eminent psychologist, calls this empathy.[8] When I feel empathy for you, I lose my need to correct you,
to teach you, to preach to you, or to judge you. Instead, I first
want to hear you out and provide a positive, supportive ground
from which you can find your way. As psychologists, we are
excited to see how many people, when listened to empathically,
find the right way on their own. But how do you listen in this
way?

First, you should be quick to listen and slow to reply. A rule
of thumb we use is that if we feel a very strong desire to interrupt
and offer a counselee some advice, we usually wait. Often the
times when you feel most sure that you have just the piece of
advice someone needs are the times you should wait and keep
your mouth shut.

It's also important to realize that listening to someone's problems is every bit as important as offering suggestions for change.
It's not time wasted. Think back to the difficult problems you've
had. Isn't it true that when you talk to someone about your
problems, the first thing you want the other person to do is to

somehow convey that he or she has clearly heard you?

You can convey that you are listening in a variety of ways. You can maintain eye contact with the other person: not staring, just moderate visual contact. You can nod your head and say yes or uh-huh to communicate that you are listening. You might lean forward in your chair.

In addition to these obvious behaviors there are also clear verbal things you can do. One major one is to be able to *summarize* what the other person has just said to you. Note how Jerry summarizes for his wife, Rose, in the following example:

Rose: Your mother came over to the house yesterday, and it was a mess. The dishes weren't done, your dirty clothes were scattered about, the kids' toys were all over the living room. I don't know why I can't get some help around here. I simply can't do all these things and get that thesis done for school too.

Jerry: I think I understand what you're saying. You feel overloaded with household chores and you'd like some help from the rest of us.

By summarizing, Jerry shows that he has been listening and helps to set the stage for clear communication by helping his wife organize the issues between them. Note also that Jerry doesn't assume that he has fully understood. He begins by saying "I think I understand." This is an invitation to Rose to clarify issues more if she feels he really doesn't understand yet.

It is a fact that most of us, especially in our close relations, think that we understand others better than we really do. In doing so, we jump to conclusions, summarize according to our biases, and are quick to judge. Take, for example, Tim, a young college student facing questions about his faith in the classroom. He tries to express his concerns to his father.

Tim: Dad, it's really a struggle at college. Yesterday my sociology professor was saying that religious groups are just people who have been conditioned to hold on to outmoded rituals and superstitions that don't—

Father (interrupting): So you're going to be like so many other young people at college today! You're going to listen to a bunch of egghead humanistic professors and drop your faith just like that? Son, don't do that. Don't throw your faith away.

Now there's no question that Tim's father is concerned about him. But in his zeal, he hasn't listened to his son. Tim hasn't said anything about throwing his faith away. His father has presumed that. In fact, by interrupting, Tim's father has missed whatever point Tim is really trying to make. To summarize well, you must listen well.

In addition to summarizing the content of another person's message, a good listener is able to *reflect feelings.*

Embedded in the serious messages of most people we listen to are a variety of feelings. Most often these feelings are not expressed clearly. A good listener tries to become attuned to these subtle expressions of feelings, label the feelings, and then reflect those feelings back to the speaker.

Frank is listening to his elderly mother talk about Frank's father, who is in poor health. Note how Frank listens and reflects.

Mother (with intensity): I don't know what I'm going to do with your father! The doctor told him to limit his physical activity, but he still overdoes it. Yesterday he tried to do some gardening outside and came in fifteen minutes later looking as white as a sheet.

Frank: You're really worried that Dad is going to hurt himself?

Mother: That's right! It worries me to death (crying). I tell him to stop it, but he doesn't pay any attention to me. He goes right on.

Frank: You get to feeling really helpless when you're unable to have an effect on his behavior.

Mother: Oh, my, yes! I'm just going to have to figure out some way to get through to him.

This conversation is not over, of course. Much remains to be done to deal with the issue at hand. But note what has occurred so far. Frank, listening with great care to his mother, has been able accurately to detect and reflect back the inner feelings that she is expressing to him (worry, helplessness). By doing so, he has helped his mother identify her true feelings (the first step toward dealing with them effectively) and has clearly let her know that he is listening keenly to the deepest parts of her communication. He has also encouraged his mother to express herself even more to him and has established a groundwork of trust in which they can look for solutions together.

SOLVING PROBLEMS ASSERTIVELY

In chapter 5, we discussed how I-messages can help in a variety of situations. We hope you've had a chance to discover the helpfulness of I-messages in your own life.

However, you've probably also discovered that knowing how to use I-messages is not always enough. This is especially true when the feelings within yourself are especially strong or when the problem between you and the other person is complex.

That's when you need to know something about creative problem solving. Creative problem solving can help you take a long look at yourself, the various issues that make up your problem, possible solutions to the problem, and ways to reach resolutions.

LOOK AT YOURSELF

The first step in assertive problem solving is to look inward and come to grips with any negative thoughts and feelings you may have. Often these negative thoughts and feelings are related to basic insecurities. They are often powerful and significant. They encompass themes like love, possession, and power. They are themes that most of us have grown up with from our earliest days. A few examples will clearly illustrate these kinds of thoughts to you.

"I'm afraid I'll lose her love."

"I can't let him get the upper hand or he'll crush me."

"I don't know whether I can stand her rejection."

These are all forms of negative self-talk, but they go deeper in that they cut to the core of our inner feelings.

Out of these thoughts can come fear, anger, resentment, and other emotions. Often these emotions are much stronger than the real problem situation warrants. The more intense they become, the more they will affect the way we handle problems. They may cause us to avoid problem solving altogether, to make comments inadvertently that we will regret, or to go into a rage and say whatever rolls off our tongue.

A man told us this story:

> A number of years ago, I found myself at odds with the manager at the place where I was working. It seemed that I could do nothing right for this man. My work was criticized incessantly, despite the fact that it had seemed all right before. With time, I began to experience a growing fear about the situation. I wondered if I would lose my job and what that would do to my work record and my personal security. At times I would feel angry. I wanted to tell that boss a thing or two. Realizing the intensity of my feelings, I held back from saying anything to him save on one occasion, when I slipped and made a critical remark that my boss threw right back at me.
>
> Later, I got my feelings off my chest with one of my wisest and best friends. After hearing me out with great care, he said, "You know, in situations like this, there's one thing I always try and remember. My deepest security is in Christ, and no one can take that away from me."
>
> At first I wanted to say, "I know that already." But then I thought carefully about his words. In this instance, did I really know, at the deepest level, that my security was in Christ? I began to remind myself of Jesus' great love for me and that this is his free gift, which no one can take away from me. I reminded myself that no matter what happens to me on this earth, I am secure in his love. My self-esteem is safe through him.
>
> As I did that, a new peace began to settle over me during the course of the next several days. I was not totally without some turmoil over my situation, but I felt a sense of inner peace about who

I was. I didn't expect God to solve all my problems, but as the intensity of my emotions subsided, I was able to think more clearly about my situation and use creative self-talk.

I began to think of ways I might be able to speak to my boss and gain at least some resolution of the problem between us.

This story illustrates the power we Christians have through our faith in God. He is there to help us. We can count on him to help us calm our inner insecurities so that we can then go on to resolve the difficulty.

USE I-MESSAGES

Once you have dealt with yourself, you can present your concern to the person in the form of an I-message. We have discussed how to do this in chapter 5. However, one additional word needs to be said. When you deal with complex problems, it is generally most helpful to frame your I-messages as open-ended invitations to negotiate. In other words, instead of *stating* a solution to the problem, ask the other person to join you in *finding* a solution. In this way, you are more likely to reach an agreement.

SUMMARIZE PROBLEMS

Don't be too quick to find a solution until you're sure you both know what the problem is. Though it may seem awkward at first, it's often helpful for each person to summarize what he or she thinks the problem is. Unless you both agree on exactly what the problem is, you won't find a solution. Look back at the active listening skills described earlier for specific ways to do this.

BRAINSTORM SOLUTIONS

Once you have fully defined the problem, you're ready to look at solutions. Organizational psychologists tell us that one of the best ways to do this is through "brainstorming." In brainstorming, each person thinks up as many solutions as possible. It is often helpful to write ideas down on paper. A cardinal rule of brainstorming is that, as you are doing it, neither of you should throw out or discard any of the solutions you've come up with. Discarding ideas during brainstorming hampers creativity, bogs down the process, and increases the chances of a fight. At this stage, you're just trying to record all possible solutions, even if some of them seem farfetched.

EVALUATE THE SOLUTIONS

Now is the time to look at which solutions are workable and which are not. Try to narrow your brainstorming list down to a reasonable number of alternatives that seem to both of you as though they might succeed. From these, pick a solution that you both can agree to try. Realize that this means you will have to be ready internally and externally to compromise. The solution you pick will probably not have everything you would like, but it will include some of your wishes.

TRY A SOLUTION AND EVALUATE RESULTS

Once you have chosen an alternative, make it specific enough so that it can be implemented and then try it. Then set aside some time at a later date to evaluate the solution. For example, if you and your spouse agree to split the duties of disciplining the children so that they are more equitable, set a date to get back together and discuss whether or not the plan worked. An evaluation session is not a blaming session, where you attack the other person for falling short. It's a time to troubleshoot the difficulties that naturally arise when you try something new. It's also a time to encourage each other to keep working toward mutual solutions that work.

Exercise 16

When it comes to conflict situations that require assertive problem solving, most people can think of several situations already pending in their lives. That's because most of us tend to avoid resolving these situations. What unresolved situations are there in your life that could benefit from problem solving? List them in your notebook.

Now go back and note how difficult it would be for you to behave assertively in each of these situations. Use the rating scale we've used previously: *a, b,* or *c.*

7

One Month to Greater Assertiveness

In earlier chapters you've learned lots of new ideas. Now it's time to put these ideas into practice. This chapter is a one-month self-help program in assertiveness training. Each exercise is designed to be completed in one week, and you should be finished with all the assignments by the end of the month. If you do each exercise carefully, you'll be surprised by what you can do at the end of a month.

If you haven't already, now is the time to put the buddy system into practice. We hope your friend has been reading along with you. During the next month, the two of you will be able to help each other become more assertive through the exercises that follow.

If you don't have a buddy to go through the program with you, at least ask a supportive friend or relative to help you get started by doing the first exercise with you. While you can receive benefit from these exercises by doing them alone, you can receive a great deal more by working with someone else. That's because assertiveness is an interpersonal skill, as we've said, and is best learned through trying it out with other people. The best way to try it out is in relatively safe situations. By working with a buddy, you'll be able to practice your skill with another supportive person before actually using it in the real world.

Now, if you're ready, let's proceed to the exercise for the first week..

EXERCISE, WEEK 1

Contact your buddy and agree to get together at least once during this week. You should plan to spend at least two hours together. Spend the first 20 minutes discussing what you've learned so far. Has the book helped you identify things about yourself that you weren't aware of before? Tell your buddy about these things.

We want you to spend the next 70 minutes practicing your assertiveness on each other. Plan to share the time, 35 minutes apiece for the practice. Here's how:

1. Very briefly describe to your buddy a real-life situation in which you'd like to be more assertive. You might want to select one of the situations you listed in exercises 9, 11, 12, 15, and 16 in chapter 6. Don't try to pick a very difficult one for your first try.

Describe, in such a way that your buddy understands, *the situation itself, the people involved,* and *how the people are likely to communicate in the situation.* Remember to be *brief.* When people do this part, it's easy for the discussion to turn into a long-winded gripe session. You're not getting together to gripe. You simply want your buddy to understand the basic mechanics of the situation so that he or she will be able to help you with it.

2. Once you've described the situation, you and your buddy are then ready to practice or rehearse the situation as if it were actually taking place. In the rehearsal, you play yourself and your buddy will play the person with whom you are trying to be more assertive. For example, Cathy had been wanting to ask her boss for clarification of her job description for several weeks. Increasingly, her boss had been doing things that Cathy felt she was trained to do. Cathy asked her buddy, Erica, to play the part of the boss and rehearse the situation in which Cathy would ask the boss for clarification. To help Erica know how to play the boss role, Cathy explained that her boss was a very quiet man who tended to clam up when asked questions. Cathy and Erica then rehearsed the scene just as if it were really happening. (If Erica has trouble behaving like the boss at first, Cathy can coach

her a bit on how to play the role better.)

3. After rehearsing, discuss how assertive you were. Your buddy should give you feedback on the following:

Your general assertiveness. Ask your buddy to pretend to be in the shoes of the person receiving your assertive message. What would be the effect of your message on that person? Would he or she have been put off, enraged, frightened, defensive?

Your eye contact. Good eye contact as you rehearse is important. Was your eye contact direct, but without staring?

Your voice tone. Was it clear, not whining or pleading? Did the volume seem about right?

Your body language. Was your body language assertive, or was it self-effacing or aggressive? As important as your words are to assertive communication, if your body language isn't congruent with your words, you won't communicate accurately.

Buddies should be sure to give positive feedback as well as suggest areas for improvement.

4. Once you've gotten feedback from your buddy, rehearse the situation again, trying to incorporate the suggestions your buddy has made. Rehearse the situation as many times as you need to before you and your buddy are both satisfied with your behavior.

5. Change places. Now your buddy will describe a situation and rehearse it, following the same steps you did. You give feedback.

6. Practice as many situations as you both have time to do.

7. To close your time together with your buddy, have a time of verbal or silent prayer if you wish. Contemplate the reality that your self-esteem is secure in Christ and that you are deeply loved by him. Ask for wisdom, guidance, and courage to become more assertive, both for your buddy and yourself.

8. Encourage each other and promise to get back in touch in the days ahead.

After meeting with your buddy and during the remainder of the week, keep your notebook or a notepad with you at all times. Watch for situations that occur to you where being assertive could be beneficial. Jot down what the situations are, when they happen, where they happen, and any inner self-talk you find yourself having during these situations. There is no need to write a book, just brief notes that serve to remind you of your experiences. Perhaps you'll want to add some of these situations to the notebook lists you made in the exercises in chapter 6.

Now you've just read what we want you to do during the first week. Perhaps you're thinking, "This idea of rehearsing with a buddy sounds silly. I'm not an actor, and I'll feel self-conscious trying to do this."

That's all right! Everybody feels self-conscious the first few times. But believe it: Rehearsing helps!

Bert worked for a church agency and was locked in a tremendous turmoil with his boss. Every time they tried to talk about their differences, the discussion turned into a conflict without resolution.

Bert decided to rehearse the situation with his buddy. They practiced several times, and the buddy pointed out several things Bert could do to communicate better.

When Bert went back to talk with his boss, he felt more confident of what he would say and was successful in resolving the situation with his boss. In talking with his buddy later, Bert said, "I didn't think rehearsing would actually help, but when I went to see my boss, it was almost like I already knew what to do. It was like I had years of experience dealing with difficult situations like this. I felt more confident and more relaxed." Rehearsing helps. Give it a try.

EXERCISE, WEEK 2

This week you'll have an opportunity to try your new skills in some real-life situations. Don't be thwarted if you feel frightened by the prospects of behaving more assertively in real life. Most everyone feels that way. Meeting new challenges is scary, but just think of the feelings you'll have once you've succeeded.

1. Look back at exercises 9, 11, 12, 15, and 16 in chapter 6. You rated each of the problem situations *a, b,* or *c* to signify how difficult it would be for you to behave assertively in each case (*a* was slightly difficult, *b* moderately difficult, and *c* very difficult). Pick out four items that you rated *a* for slightly difficult. One of these situations might be the one you practiced last week with your buddy. During the next week, attempt to behave assertively in each of these four situations.

On a fresh page in your notebook, make a two-column REAL-LIFE COMPLETION CHART. Head the wider column *Situation Completed* and the narrower column *Number of Points.* For each situation that you attempt, note it on the chart and give yourself 5 points. Remember, your goal is to make an attempt to behave assertively whether your assertion leads to a successful outcome or not. As we mentioned before, you are only partly responsible for the outcome of the situation. The person with whom you are behaving assertively also has a part to play in determining the outcome. Your goal is simply to behave appropriately and assertively, not to make the other person respond a certain way.

2. Near the end of the week, contact your buddy by phone or in person. Report to each other on the four situations that you each attempted. Encourage and support each other where progress has been made. Where there have been problems, rehearse the situations just as you did before and give each other feedback on how to improve.

3. Once you have amassed 20 points on your completion chart, congratulate yourself by giving yourself a special treat (going out to dinner or to a show, etc.). Write the treat you plan to give yourself in the margin of your chart.

EXERCISE, WEEK 3

1. Review exercises 9, 11, 12, 15, and 16 in chapter 6. During the next week, carry out at least two situations that you rated as *b* items (moderately difficult). Also carry out at least two more situations that you rated as *a* items (slightly difficult). As you prepare to carry out these situations assertively, note the

positive and negative self-talk that you engage in. Take time to think of creative self-talk and record some of these positive thoughts in your notebook for future reference. Before attempting these situations, feel free to call your buddy to rehearse if you need to. Record each situation you attempt on the completion chart. For each *b* item attempted (whether the outcome is successful or not) give yourself 10 points on the chart. For each *a* item, give yourself 5 points.

2. Watch for a spontaneous opportunity to behave assertively this week. Life has a way of presenting situations to you on the spur of the moment that could benefit from your assertiveness. When you are able to respond assertively in one of these situations (whether you have a successful outcome or not), record the situation on the completion chart and give yourself 10 points.

3. Near the end of the week, call your buddy and share progress reports with each other. Resolve to pray for each other during the week ahead.

4. After you have amassed at least 35 points on your completion chart for the week, congratulate yourself with a special treat. Write the treat you plan to give yourself on your chart.

EXERCISE, WEEK 4

1. Look back at exercises 9, 11, 12, 15, and 16 in chapter 6. Select a *c* situation (very difficult) to try this week. Pray for wisdom and guidance. Feel free to contact your buddy, discuss the situation, and rehearse it until you feel you're ready. Give yourself 15 points on your completion chart for attempting this item.

2. Attempt any other situations from the chapter 6 exercises that you'd like. Give yourself the appropriate points for attempting these situations. Watch for spontaneous situations in which to behave assertively and give yourself points for these also.

3. Contact your buddy near the week's end and give each other encouragement and support.

4. Give yourself a special treat when you have totaled at least 35 points for the week. Write the treat on your chart.

BEYOND WEEK 4

You're on your way now! By this time you've done some great things you probably never thought you could do.

Now it's up to you. You know how to do the exercises, and you can keep doing them according to the pace and format that's most helpful for you. Catch yourself being more assertive in everyday situations and congratulate yourself. Give yourself points for attempting assertive situations and set up your own system for receiving special treats that's appropriate for you (and your pocketbook or waistline!).

Keep the following list in mind as you work to behave more assertively. You might even want to type the list on a separate sheet of paper and carry it with you in your purse or billfold as a reminder.

• Remember the key parts to an assertive communication. These include being open and honest, respecting the other person, using I-messages, being brief, and negotiating as appropriate.

• Use creative self-talk. Watch out for negative self-talk.

• Congratulate yourself liberally for small improvements. Most of us spend far too much time criticizing ourselves and far too little time feeling good about our growth.

• Remember that the person who never makes an attempt never loses, but that person never wins either. If you want to succeed, you will have to make an attempt at behaving more assertively.

• Beware the feeling that you *must* be assertive in every situation that life brings you. There are times when you may want to be nonassertive. The important thing is having the freedom to choose to be assertive or not.

• Maintain contact with your buddy.

• Pray. Reflect that God loves you and that, through Christ, you are declared worthy. Relax in prayer. Contemplate and request wisdom and maturity to deal with the conflicts that you face.

8

Being Assertive in the Midst of Conflict

If you haven't yet done the exercises in the last chapter, go back and do them. If you have, continue reading.

We trust that as you did the exercises and lived your life this past month you also experienced at least a few situations where you felt frustrated in your attempts to apply the assertive skills you've learned. More likely than not, these difficulties arose in situations where you felt a good deal of conflict, the kinds of situations we considered under "assertive problem solving" in chapter 6.

In this chapter we have a bit more to say about being assertive in the midst of conflict. This chapter is part review and encouragement and part new information. When you're in the middle of real conflict, it's easy to forget some of the things you've learned. You also may find yourself wanting more help. This chapter should be useful on both counts.

Conflicts are not just everyday situations. Conflicts are like wartime—those exceptional times when we feel we are fighting for our very existence, when we feel desperate and threatened. Conflicts require real courage and effort if one is to be assertive.

This may not sound unusual if you have ever been in a fight. You may have memories of sudden feelings, quick reactions, and impulses that amazed you and seemed to come instinctively, without much effort or forethought. To be sure, conflicts often call forth strength and combativeness we didn't know we had. Just as common is the tendency to wilt, fade away, and run. No doubt, many of us have these memories too! We all have fled as well as fought!

However, being assertive during these times is something other than fighting or fleeing. Remember, to be assertive means that we do not give up—on ourselves or on others. When we fight back we are engaged in a win-lose struggle. We are attempting to preserve our existence even if we have to annihilate the other person. Of course, murder is very rare in fights. However, just because no one gets killed does not change the fact that we have murderous thoughts when we are fighting. This is aggressiveness, not assertiveness.

The same is true when we flee the scene of a fight or give in to a threat. We give up on ourselves and our opinions. In effect, we are saying, "You win; I lose." It should go without saying that this is not assertiveness either.

Assertiveness means not giving up on yourself and not giving up on the other person. This is hard to do during conflict. That is why we say that assertiveness during conflict requires real courage and effort.

JOB: A GOOD EXAMPLE

Job is a good example of a person who was assertive during exceptional conflict. In the biblical story, the devil brought grave misfortune on Job. The devil was convinced that Job would give in when the going got tough. Not so; Job remained faithful. More importantly, Job remained assertive.

> My dispute is with God, not you;
>   I want to argue my case with him.
> . . . .
> Be quiet and give me a chance to speak,
>   and let the results be what they will.
> I am ready to risk my life.
> I've lost all hope, so what if God kills me?
>   I am going to state my case to him.
> It may even be that my boldness will save me,
>   since no wicked man would dare to face God.
> Now listen to my words of explanation.

> I am ready to state my case,
>   because I know I am in the right.
> . . . .
> Let me ask for two things; agree to them,
>   and I will not try to hide from you;
>   stop punishing me, and don't crush me with terror.
> Speak first, O God, and I will answer.
>   Or let me speak, and you answer me.
>   (Job 13:3, 13–18, 20–22)

The translation of the well-known fifteenth verse in the King James Bible, "Though he slay me, yet will I trust in him," is a bit different here, but the meaning is still there. Job refused to lie down and be passive. He did not flee from the conflict. He trusted God and he trusted himself.

This truth comes through loudly and clearly. Job did not back away. He stayed in the relationship and pleaded his case. He considered himself important and worthy enough to contend with God even though his life was in danger. This is conflict assertiveness at its best!

SOME MODERN EXAMPLES

We, like Job, are in conflict from time to time. We say "in conflict" because we, like Job, sometimes feel desperate and threatened. As contrasted with those times in which we may feel some stress or frustration, conflict experiences are those times when we are so upset our self-esteem seems at point zero. Some examples are:

- When a parent has a splitting headache and can't get the baby to stop crying
- When a driver gets stopped for speeding and has a flat tire all in the same day
- When a salesperson is chastised for not meeting a quota that everyone else met
- When a husband gets fired from his job and his wife complains that he is lazy
- When children fail in school and must explain to their parents

- When a boss files a poor evaluation report on an employee in spite of sickness in the family
- When a husband and wife argue late into the night and one of them threatens divorce

These are all Job-like situations. What they have in common with Job is the threat people feel and their sense that the situation is out of control.

We define conflict as that point in our relationships with others when we become so frightened and upset that neither the issue before us nor the people with whom we are relating become as important to us as surviving and maintaining our own self-esteem. This sense of fright may have little to do with the actual threat that the situation poses. Rarely are we physically threatened. Most of the time it is psychological survival that is at stake. But in many ways, this is just as important.

WHAT CAN WE DO?

What can we do when we go into conflict? We hope we will learn to do what Job did: Be assertive. This is the Win-Win alternative. However, being assertive is only one of the options. There are at least three other ways of reacting to conflict. These are called the Fighting, the Surrendering, and the Escaping alternatives. They correspond respectively to Win-Lose, Lose-Win, and Lose-Leave ways of handling conflicts. We need to be clear about these other options and not confuse them with assertion.

FIGHTING

We have often thought that the fighting, or Win-Lose, way of dealing with the threat of conflict is like riding forth in an armored tank. Since conflicts are like battlefields, riding over another person in a tank is an apt image. Few people can stand up to tanks, and that is just what the tank drivers intend. They intend both to win and to make others lose! In fact, if it takes annihilating the other person in the argument, that will just have to happen. The stakes are too high to take a chance.

Fighting is probably the most common way to react to conflict. It is often confused with assertion, but they are different, as you will see. People fight for their lives and only give up after being defeated. Until they lose they intend to win, regardless of what it takes. This is why fighting is called the Win-Lose way: I win, you lose.

One newly married couple had both been married before. They brought up their earlier marriages to each other constantly. They were both fighters. They would get their feelings hurt and attack each other. What happened one evening in a local restaurant was typical of the way they handled conflict.

Earlier that day, Inez, the first wife, had chanced to visit her former parents-in-law as they were looking at some photos of the newlyweds. "How do you think Inez liked our pictures?" Sharon, the new wife, asked. "I told you I don't want to talk about Inez. You're always bringing up Inez. You've got a one-track mind," the husband answered.

Then the fight began. She got defensive and he counterattacked by suggesting that she had made a bad choice in her first husband. She got so angry she threw a fork at him. The evening ended by Sharon walking out of the restaurant and going home by herself. He got in his car and drove around for several hours.

See if you can remember a time when you reacted as if you were in combat fighting a mortal enemy. Write down the occasion in your notebook.

How did you handle your feelings? Write that in your notebook too.

SURRENDER

A second way of handling the threat of conflict is by surrendering. It is the opposite of the fighting approach. When one surrenders, one gives up and lets the other person win. This is the reason that surrendering is termed Lose-Win: I lose, you win. However, we should not forget that when we are in conflict we often feel the urge to win back some good feelings about ourselves. Thus, even when we surrender we may really be saying to other people, "You are right and I am wrong. Now, please like me!"

If we can't maintain our self-esteem by winning, we hope to maintain it by letting others have their way with us. Some have called surrendering "white-flag behavior." Although we lose the battle, we hope to win the war by surrendering; we hope we will be accepted, pitied, and nurtured even though we lost the argument. Unfortunately, when we do this, we put our self-esteem in the hands of others, and if they don't accept us, we feel totally devastated.

Sam was in his thirties when he came for counsel. He was a mild-mannered, sensitive person who had been promoted to the position of head teller in his bank. About six months before he came for help, a new manager had been appointed at the bank where he worked. From the beginning it seemed as if Sam could not please his new boss. Sam's self-esteem was threatened, but, not knowing what to do about it, he just took it. He did not talk back, and he tried to please his boss—to no avail. When he came for counsel he was a beaten man. He had given up.

Most of us have surrendered from time to time. We fear we will not win, so we decide to surrender. Think back and describe in your notebook a time when you gave in or surrendered. How did you react?

ESCAPE

A third way in which we handle the threat of conflict is to escape from the event. By escaping, persons soften the impact by pretending the experience was not important anyway. This is done by the well-known psychological process called "denial." We cushion the impact of the situation by denying its importance and by saying to ourselves, "Oh, well, I didn't care anyway; it doesn't matter at all." We have often thought of this escaping reaction as "let's get the heck out of here" behavior.

Escaping is called the Leave-Lose option: I leave, I lose. We leave the scene (either physically or in our minds) and, by leaving, lose any chance of winning.

It should go without saying that this is a pretty desperate alternative. We do this when we decide we cannot maintain our self-esteem by fighting or even by surrendering. It's as if we decide there is no hope. So we walk away and take the loss, as it were. We hope to regain our security by saying we don't care.

Elizabeth was a clerk at a factory. She had to work in close cooperation with Laura, who sat at the next desk. One day Elizabeth was late in getting an order to Laura for processing. Laura retaliated by giving Elizabeth the cold shoulder and not talking to her. The two of them would hand the necessary papers back and forth, but for the next week this was the extent of their communication. At the end of the week, Elizabeth couldn't take it anymore. Despite the fact that she loved her job otherwise, the pay was good, and she had no other job prospects, she quit. She told herself that quitting was no big deal and she really didn't need the job anyway. Elizabeth escaped.

We have all probably escaped at one time or another. Think of a time when you escaped and write it down in your notebook. How did you escape?

ASSERTION

A fourth way to handle conflict is assertion. It does not intentionally hurt other persons as fighting does. It does not give in to others as surrender does. It does not run away as escaping does. Assertion stays *in* the relationship with others and stays *with* the viewpoints that are being challenged. It is the Win-Win alternative.

In a controversy with his father, Wendell, a senior in high school, provided a good example of assertion in the face of conflict. Late one Friday evening he was ticketed for speeding on the way home from a date. His father got very angry and gave him a stern lecture. Wendell was embarrassed and humiliated, since this was the first time he had gotten a speeding ticket. The morning after this confrontation with his father, Wendell decided to write this letter:

Dear Dad,

I got a speeding ticket last night, and I was wrong. You were right in being mad at me. I betrayed your trust in me. But I want you to know that I think you were too harsh. I think you should put last night in context. I am trying to find my place and it is not easy. Maybe I should go out on my own. Maybe I'd do better to leave. But I don't want to yet. I love you and want to please you. Let's talk when you have time.

Love,
Wendell

This is assertion at its best!

Can you think of a time when you were assertive in the face of conflict? Write it down in your notebook.

How did you assert yourself?

Fighting, surrender, and escape all mean rejection; assertion means affirmation—affirmation of oneself and affirmation of others. Assertion has been called "confronting with caring." It means having enough courage to stand up and enough care to stand with. Our hope is that you will want to be caring enough and courageous enough to learn to assert yourself in the face of conflict. Our confidence is that you can do it and that you do not need to hurt, give in, or run away—as many people do. A set of steps for becoming more assertive in conflict follows.

STEPS IN CONFLICT ASSERTION

When we are in conflict, we are having a difficult experience. The first thing to do is to calm down and get some control over ourselves. This is called "conflict reduction." It is necessary to reduce the conflict in ourselves before we can even think about how to assert ourselves.

How can we calm down when we are feeling so threatened? We Christians can calm ourselves down by reminding ourselves that our self-worth is not based on what others think of us or on whether we win or lose an argument. John 3:16 is only one of many scriptural passages that state the truth about God's love for us: "For God loved the world so much that he gave his only

Son, so that everyone who believes in him may not die but have eternal life." As Paul reminded us in Romans 8:37, "in all these things we have complete victory through him who loved us!" We can sit down and remind ourselves that our security is in Christ. You will remember that this was an important step in assertive problem solving, which we discussed in chapter 6. Reminding ourselves of God's love and our security in him is even more important when we are trying to handle conflict.

Of course, this will involve our getting away from the conflict situation, if only for a minute. It's very hard to calm down in the midst of battle. Retreating in order to recall God's love for us is the first step.

In addition to calming down by reminding ourselves of the self-esteem that comes from our faith, we should quiet our bodies by breathing quietly and deeply and going through several minutes of relaxation.

After we have calmed down we should then return to the situation and enter afresh into the encounter. At this point, we can take the next step, which is to state our case to the other person. Job and Wendell illustrated this step very well. Job stated to God that he wanted an audience with him. Wendell wrote to his father that he wanted to talk. If persons want to be assertive in conflict, they should state to the other person what they want to do. This is important. It should be said that this does not necessarily mean that we talk about the issues that provoked the conflict. It does mean stating that we want to go back into the interaction. It also means that we suggest *how* we want the discussion to proceed.

After calming down and making statements about what we want to happen, we can better apply the steps toward assertive problem solving that were described earlier (see chapter 6). These are:

Using I-messages to take responsibility for your role in the situation

Trying to restate the problem in terms that acknowledge the issue as well as recognize why everyone has become so upset

Brainstorming ways to handle the problem while honoring the people involved (yourself included)

Entering back into the relationship with a solution in mind —in other words, taking the risk of trying again

Continuing to remind yourself, throughout the whole process, that God loves and forgives you—for your best as well as your worst.

In summary, conflict is a special type of situation. We must *reduce* the conflict in ourselves before we can be assertive. By reminding ourselves of the security we have in God's love, by calming our bodies down, and by stating to our protagonist that we want to talk again under a new set of conditions—by taking these steps we can proceed to be assertive in the same way that we were when we were not in conflict. In these ways we can be caring and courageous. We can stand up for our convictions at the same time that we stand with others who provoke and frustrate us.

Think ahead to a time when you will be in conflict. Describe it in your notebook. Now, plan a written strategy for being assertive, following the steps outlined. What will you do?

9

Being Assertive at Church

Most of what we have been saying about assertiveness has pertained to your behavior with one or two other persons. What about assertiveness in groups? This is a different issue. We all know that sometimes we feel secure in a one-to-one interaction but feel very nervous when several other persons are involved. In this chapter we want to talk about how to be assertive in these situations too. We are convinced that people can learn not to be afraid in groups. We are hopeful that reading this chapter will help you get over your timidity or your aggressiveness. We think you can become as assertive with several people as you are with only one or two.

We have titled this chapter "Being Assertive at Church" because church is one of those places where we must relate to groups of people. Rarely is church a place where we are with only one other person. We worship in sanctuaries where pews are filled with people. We attend classes where discussions are held in which many people participate. We serve on committees where plans are made by ten or more people. We sing in choirs, we engage in projects, we eat at banquets, we meet on boards —all events where groups are involved.

Of course, church is only one of those places in life where we have to relate to others. What is true of church is true of schools, neighborhood associations, clubs, sports teams, on-the-job task forces, community projects, and travel tour groups. Each presents an opportunity for assertiveness. Each presents an opportunity for us to be timid or aggressive. Each, like the church, provokes in us different kinds of feelings from those we have when we are talking with just one or two other persons.

So what you learn in this chapter can apply to all those groups of which you are a part. We have chosen the church because most of you belong to a church. You will easily recognize the examples we consider. You will be able to apply these ideas next Sunday. But you will also be able to take these ideas and apply them in your everyday experience in other places.

THE LAST TIME YOU WERE AT CHURCH . . .

Shut your eyes and think about the last time you attended church. See if you can recapture the feelings you had as you left home, while you traveled, and when you arrived.

You probably left a situation at home in which you were talking to only one or two persons, your family or friends. You were on your way to a situation where you would meet many people and have to interact with them.

As you think back, what were you feeling in this travel time between home and church? Did your feelings change? Were you looking forward to being there or did you have some anxiety?

If you are anything like most people we know, you felt both excited and anxious—all at the same time. Church excites us and church depresses us! Often our feelings change radically when we go out in public. Don't be surprised if you can't remember these feelings well. Many of us have become so accustomed to them that they are hard to recall. However, you can probably recognize them if you just relax and reflect about your last trip to church.

Take your memory one step farther.

Recall arriving at church and going toward the door. Think about the first persons that you met. Were they friends, strangers, acquaintances? How did you feel? What did you say?

Once again, continue your recollection by thinking about what you did next.

You were probably at church to attend some meeting. Imagine yourself going to that meeting. Where did you sit? What did you do? Were you a leader or a participant? How did you feel?

Think about how you behaved. Were you timid, or aggressive, or assertive? Did you stay the same throughout the meeting, or did you change from time to time? Did you relax, or did you become tense?

This memory should provide a basis on which to think about how to become more assertive in groups. We hope it gave you a sense of how you react in these situations. If you remembered being always assertive and never timid or aggressive, you probably don't need to read further in this chapter. However, if you found yourself having mixed feelings and experiencing less security than you would like, this chapter is for you. As you well know from earlier chapters, our conviction is that the more assertive and the less timid or aggressive you can be, the more fulfilled you will feel from the time you spend in groups. The following example illustrates this change in a young woman we know.

THE GIRL WHO CAME IN FROM THE COLD

The young woman in this case joined a church in Hollywood, California, because she was lonely and wanted a group to which she could belong. The church had very strong and authoritative leadership, and she followed faithfully. She lived in one of the church's houses, attended Bible study weekly, and went along quietly with her friends as they evangelized on the streets of the city. She had little to say in church meetings. Her behavior could best be described as timid.

As time went on, her self-confidence grew. She got a raise at work. Her duties gave her more responsibility. She began to feel that she would like to speak up more in Bible study and help determine where they went on Saturdays. She wanted to be more assertive, yet she did not know how. She felt her church would not like it if she spoke out and expressed her opinions. She became restless and began to complain about a number of things at the church. She considered going elsewhere but hesi-

tated because "they" wouldn't like it. Yet she continued to think
that if she stayed she would have to be her old timid self.

We named her "the girl who came in from the cold" because
of her reason for joining the church. It could also be said she
was "the girl who was afraid of the cold," because of her reasons
for staying.

WHY ARE GROUPS SO FRIGHTENING?

The illustration of the girl who came in from the cold may
be more typical than we think. It is easy to feel sorry for her and
yet not recognize that many of us feel that way about groups.
Why are groups so upsetting? There are several reasons.

The first reason people often give for finding groups or crowds
upsetting is the sheer number of people involved. How many
times have you heard it said, "You can never guess how they
will all react." What is meant is that there are just too many
faces to read, too many eyes to look into, too many reactions to
judge, too many moods to comprehend. When persons interact
with each other individually they can focus on the other's tone
of voice, facial expression, body posture, and the look in their
eyes. On that basis they can decide what to say or do. But
crowds are too complex. There are so many people involved,
they make us feel insecure. We can't predict how everybody will
react. Take the case of Martin, for example. He drives an eight-
een-wheeler transport truck. He has a co-worker who shares the
driving on a run from Milwaukee to Atlanta and back. Martin
is known as energetic, forthright, opinionated, and capable. No
one would ever call him timid, yet that is exactly how he behaves
on Sunday at church. If you saw him you would ask, "Is this
the same man who drives the truck?" When asked why he never
said anything in his church school class or why he waited for
people to shake his hand at the coffee hour, Martin replied,
"There are just too many people there for me to feel comfortable. The safest thing for me is to be quiet."

The second reason people give for finding groups upsetting is
that there is not enough time for everybody to be heard. Their

meetings are always limited by a certain number of minutes. If someone has something to say, there is the danger that there will not be enough time for a full explanation of what that person means. As is often said, "You can't count on groups to understand what you say—they will cut you off and leave you stranded." So people who go to group meetings sometimes do one of two things. They either force people to listen to them by talking loud and long or they just keep quiet.

Take the example of Gail. A more considerate, nurturing, understanding, and helpful person would be hard to find. She was the mother of five and a nurse at the local junior high school. Yet in the Christian education committee at her church she is known as "the bull in sheep's clothing." She has an opinion on every issue and fights to persuade others to support her position. She becomes hostile and raises her voice at the slightest provocation. If asked why she acts this way at church when she has the reputation of being a very different person at home and at school, she would say, "Church is different. They never listen. If I waited on them to ask me how I felt, it would never happen. The meeting would be over before I had a chance to say anything."

The third reason sometimes given for why groups are upsetting is that leaders don't care. Leaders don't care about what? Leaders don't care about members, it is often said. Sometimes leaders are seen as only caring about programs and projects. People feel ignored and discounted. The word "steamrolling" is used to describe the way leaders push things through and use their power to get their way. Members who feel they are not important will either become docile or obstruct the group. This situation is fairly common in churches. Church leaders often speak as if they have special insight into eternal truths, giving lay people the idea that they do not know enough to speak up. Yet they often have opinions and feel slighted when they try to express them.

Take the case of Horatio. Horatio sells shoes at a large department store. He has worked at this job for over fifteen years and knows a great deal about materials and styles. He has been the one to go to New York and purchase the yearly supply of shoes for his store for the last five seasons. He also knows a lot about the Bible. He trained as leader of a Bible study series and has taught a Bible class for several years. Yet in elders' meetings he is unpredictable. At times he will act as if he is half asleep, while at other times he will interrupt a speaker and express his opinion in a boisterous and aggressive manner. When asked why he acts the way he does, Horatio would say, "Sometimes it's just not worth the effort. The pastor knows what he wants and gets it. We don't really have any say. Occasionally I have to speak up and force my way in. Otherwise those in charge would just run over us."

The fourth reason people are afraid of groups is that they get saddled with responsibility they don't want. Sometimes when they speak out, they get asked to take some job and the group pressures them into accepting it—even when they don't want to do it! This has been called the "saddle effect." Just as a horse may have a saddle put on his back when he would rather stay in the corral, so people often get responsibility thrust on them. Groups upset such people; they don't think they can stand up to the pressure to get overinvolved and take too much responsibility.

Take Martha, for example. She is a vice-president at one of the banks in her hometown. She is known as a very capable executive and an astute businesswoman. At church she is a Milquetoast. She hardly ever speaks up in meetings of the board of trustees, of which she is a member. This mystifies the pastor, who recommended she be appointed a trustee because of her business background. If you ask her why she is so quiet at church, she would answer, "Every time I give my opinion they ask me to chair some committee. I always give in even when I know that I'm overcommitting myself. I just can't seem to keep my cool when they are all looking at me. I'd rather keep quiet, even though it looks as if I don't have any opinions."

These four illustrations are sad but true. Most of us have known persons like Martin, Gail, Horatio, and Martha. Most of us can easily identify with the four reasons groups upset people.

Exercise 17

Think back to the last time you went to church. This is the same memory you recalled earlier in this chapter. Were you the same person you usually are away from church? Did you behave differently there from the way you behave when you are speaking to a family member or friend? What reason would you give, if any, for what you did? In your notebook, describe exactly what you did and then write your reason for doing it.

Would you characterize your behavior as timid, aggressive, or assertive? Remember, the more assertive behavior the better, and the less timid or aggressive behavior the better. Also recall that timid behavior is defined as denying your own opinions and giving all the power to others. Aggressive behavior is defined as taking all the power into your own hands and forcing others to do things your way. Assertive behavior is defined as expressing yourself forcefully but being willing to share power with others.

WHAT CAN BE DONE ABOUT GROUPS?

What can be done about groups? The answer is nothing and everything. All the reasons given for being afraid of groups are true. Groups seem not to change. They do have many people in them. They do have to meet time schedules. Leaders do push programs. Groups are complex and hard to figure. Group meetings do end without everyone's having their say or being understood. Members do feel they are misused. Nothing can be done about groups.

Yet everything can be done about groups. We are not as powerless as we sometimes think. Groups do not rule us; we can rule groups. In the final analysis, most of the reasons as to why groups are upsetting are, in fact, excuses for not taking the risk of being assertive. As some psychologists put it, "When we say 'I can't' we usually mean 'I won't.'" So if we are timid or aggressive in groups, it probably is because we have decided we won't be assertive. It probably means we have decided it would be too hard, take too much energy, or be too risky.

We can only say that the rewards for being assertive in groups and at church are great and that once you try it you will never want to return to being timid or aggressive again. It is like the young woman introduced to high society in *My Fair Lady*. She never wanted to go back to being a flower girl. So it is with learning to be assertive.

The situation of the girl who came in from the cold illustrates this. Once her self-respect began to rise, and she began to know what it was like to express herself, she was no longer satisfied with being a timid follower at church. She felt a strong need to assert herself. And this need would not go away.

We helped her learn to become more assertive, and she decided to stay in her congregation. She did not join another church, nor did she remain unhappy and complaining. She learned to be assertive, and so can you! She is much more satisfied now, even though her pastor and other church leaders still exert strong control over what the members do. She illustrates the truth of the old saying, "A person can if a person will."

RULES FOR GROUP ASSERTIVENESS

Here are five rules for becoming more assertive in groups. We believe that if you follow and practice these rules you will succeed.

1. First, you must be willing to try. This may sound silly, because you wouldn't have read this far in this chapter unless you wanted to become more assertive at church and in other groups. However, wanting something and being willing to try a new way may be two different things.

The girl who came in from the cold wanted to change, and she was *willing* to try. Are you? Don't treat this question lightly. Changing what you are accustomed to do is hard—particularly what you are accustomed to do in groups. But know this: We are confident that if you are willing to try you will find the way to change.

2. The second rule for becoming more assertive in groups is to relax. It is well known that we often do things to reduce our anxiety and make ourselves feel better. As we have shown, groups are upsetting. They make us anxious. So we need to learn to relax whenever we are in the midst of a group of people. There are two good ways of doing this.

As you walk up to a group, take a deep breath and smile (either outwardly or inwardly) and tell yourself, as you breathe out, "My body is calm and my mind is awake." Do this at least twice every time you breathe out. Slowly breathe in and out several times. This can be done no matter where you are. It will take no more than a minute or two.

You can also become relaxed by remembering that you are in no danger. This can be done quietly by repeating one or two Bible verses, such as Isaiah 26:3–4: "You, LORD, give perfect peace to those who keep their purpose firm and put their trust in you. Trust in the LORD forever; he will always protect us." These verses will calm you because they remind you of your true security. Your true security comes from God, not from the group.

Relaxing yourself will make it possible for you to take the last three steps toward becoming more assertive in groups. These steps are: stand up, speak up, and shut up. You may have heard them before. They are the humorous rules for public speaking, but they are also rules for becoming more assertive in groups.

3. "Stand up" means "Don't hold back," or "Enter in." It means "Have an opinion," or "Get excited." If it is true, as we think it is, that groups upset people, the usual reaction is to be cautious and hold back—be timid. Of course, as we noted, some people do the opposite: they become overly brazen and aggressive. However, we think those who are aggressive are the exceptions. Most people take the timid route. So overcoming the timidness is an important step. Stand up!

Standing up is not easy to do, but it is far easier when you have set your mind to try and when you have relaxed yourself. The following are examples of what it's like to stand up.

Standing up is when:

• You walk right up and sit in one of the front seats
• You wiggle your way into the center of a group so you can hear what's being said
• You take notes on a pad about the opinions that are being expressed
• You keep your mind on what's going on
• You turn to face persons who are speaking from the audience
• You raise your hand to express your opinion
• You take a stand on the issues and do not abstain on votes

These are only a few examples of what it means to stand up. You can probably think of more.

Exercise 18

Think about the next time you will be in a group and list in your notebook one or two things you could do to "stand up."

4. The fourth step in becoming more assertive in groups is "speak up." Standing up has to do with putting yourself in the place where you can "speak up." Speaking up is what you say or do once you are there. Both are important. You can't speak up if you haven't stood up. Nor is it good to stand up if you don't follow through and speak up.

To speak up means to put your thoughts into words. It means to have an opinion, make a judgment, give voice to your feelings, say what you think, take a side, offer a statement. It is, of course, easier to say what not to do, but speaking up is a positive, not a negative, act. It is something you *do,* not something you *stop* doing. Being assertive means that you may say something even though you know that it may not be the "perfect" thing to say and even though you take a risk in saying it. So the fourth rule for group assertiveness is "speak up."

5. The final rule for group assertiveness is "shut up." "How can you suggest such a strange rule as 'shut up'?" someone might ask. "Aren't we interested in people speaking up more

than shutting up, being vocal rather than quiet?" they might add. The answer is, "Of course, but. . . ." Those who don't know when to shut up become aggressive and overbearing. Knowing when to stop and listen to others is a key skill in learning how to be assertive.

Why? There are several reasons. It is helpful to know when one is about to step over the line from stating an opinion to having to have one's way. This is the fine line that separates standing up for one's rights and becoming hostile and combative.

Again, knowing when to shut up is helpful because it means we believe other people's ideas are just as important as our own. Notice we did not say that others' ideas are necessarily more *correct* than ours. We said that others' opinions are as *important* as our own. Listening to what they have to say does not mean we have to agree with them, only that we have to respect them. This is an important part of being assertive.

Furthermore, we may learn something we hadn't thought of before if we shut up and listen. While we have a perfect right to our opinion, and while we are not called upon to change our ideas when we shut up, we may hear some point of view or some facts we hadn't considered before. As the old saying goes, "Two heads are better than one." And they are. The decision we reach together may be better than the decision we could have reached by ourselves.

So, being assertive means to shut up when we have said our piece. After speaking up we should be quiet and listen out of respect for others, in an effort to learn something new and because we want to avoid aggressiveness.

Exercise 19

In an effort to anticipate "shutting up," think ahead to a time in the next few weeks when you will be at church. Imagine yourself entering into a discussion about something. What will it be? Write your answer in your notebook.

Now imagine you have stated an opinion. Write it down.

Next, imagine that you shut up. Write down what you will do. Include your behavior, your body posture, your feelings.

You can become assertive in groups if you will. We are convinced that you will do it and feel good about it *if* you will follow the suggestions given in this chapter.

The Last Word

Congratulations! You've come to the end of this book. It's our hope that you learned some new things about being assertive. But before you put the book down, we want to remind you of a couple of things you need to know. Sometimes, when people read a book like this they get so excited about the things they learn that they do what we call "overkill." They begin to get the notion that they should *always* be assertive no matter what the situation.

The fact is, assertiveness is not something you must do, it is something you can do if you choose to. Assertiveness is not some new dogma designed to take over your life. It is simply a very effective communication tool that we hope you'll add to your other life skills.

We also hope you'll avoid seeing assertiveness as a means to get your way. Just because you are assertive doesn't mean others will always go along with you. Assertiveness is not a means to manipulate others, it is a way of communicating clearly to others. Just like anything else, assertiveness can be used for manipulation, if that's your goal. But in our book, that's not being assertive; it's really aggressive.

We know that assertiveness won't allow you to solve every problem or conflict with other people. Sometimes, conflicts aren't resolved despite your very best efforts. Remember that you're not the only person involved in solving a problem or conflict. "It takes two to tango." If you've done your very best and the other person refuses to deal with you, you can give yourself an A for effort and move on. Give yourself permission not to work every single problem out right now.

Finally, as we've said, assertiveness is a skill and, because it is a skill, it has to be practiced over and over to be learned well. Our strongest hope is that you'll keep developing your assertiveness. You can do that by reading and rereading this book. We've also included a list of some other books that can be of help to you. You may find that you want to participate in an assertiveness workshop, group, or counseling program as a way of continuing to develop your skills and work out any specific needs that you have individually. In any case, we hope you'll see assertiveness as a process that you can get better at, the more you learn and practice it.

Appendixes

Appendix A

1. *WHEN* I go out to the car in the morning and there's no gas in it,
2. *I FEEL* angry and worried;
3. *I'D LIKE* you (Jeff) to make sure it has at least half a tank of gas in it after you use it.

Appendix B

Feeling Words

brave	tender	suspicious
peaceful	angry	blessed
intelligent	adventurous	apathetic
elated	ashamed	ambivalent
delighted	envious	worried
joyful	bitter	thankful
hopeful	hating	humble
amused	disliked	pained
warm	sick	adoring
happy	hurt	frustrated
appreciated	lovely	generous
consoled	depressed	flippant
awed	hopeless	liking
infatuated	embarrassed	caring
passionate	humiliated	concerned

inspired	afraid	aloof
proud	terrified	alive
relaxed	confused	trusting
loved	anxious	calm
contented	tense	nostalgic
sad	strong	irritable
annoyed	sullen	reverent

Notes

1. Edward A. Charlesworth and Ronald G. Nathan, *Stress Management: A Comprehensive Guide to Wellness* (Biobehavioral Press, 1981).
2. Leonard Berkowitz, *Roots of Aggression: A Re-examination of the Frustration-Aggression Hypothesis* (Atherton Press, 1969).
3. William Barclay, *The Beatitudes and the Lord's Prayer for Everyman* (Harper & Row, 1975).
4. David Daube, *Civil Disobedience in Antiquity* (Edinburgh University Press, 1972).
5. Albert Ellis and Robert A. Harper, *A New Guide to Rational Living* (Wilshire Book Co., 1975).
6. Quoted in Charles L. Wallis, ed., *The Treasure Chest* (Harper & Row, 1965), p. 87.
7. Thomas Gordon, *Parent Effectiveness Training: The No-Lose Program for Raising Responsible Children* (Peter H. Wyden, 1970).
8. Carl R. Rogers, "The necessary and sufficient conditions of therapeutic personality change," *Journal of Consulting Psychology* 21: 95–103 (1957).

Further Reading

Here are several other books you might like to read. They are all useful in one way or another. Each of them can help you become even more assertive in the way we have been describing.

Alberti, Robert E., and Michael L. Emmons. *Your Perfect Right: A Guide to Assertive Living,* 4th ed. Impact Pubs. (Cal.), 1982. This is one of the original classics in the field of assertiveness training. The book contains basic ideas for developing more assertive behavior. The authors' discussion of the dangers of aggression is especially helpful. The book also contains helpful guidelines for the professional seeking to train others in assertiveness.

Augsburger, David W. *Anger and Assertiveness in Pastoral Care.* Fortress Press, 1979. Written especially to pastors, this book also has much to say about the problems of being assertive at church. The author, a prominent pastoral psychologist, discusses difficulties that pastors have in controlling their anger and in using their hostility creatively. He suggests that pastors can be aware, can channel, can assert, and can release angry energy in a manner that will build up the church, rather than tear it down.

———. *Caring Enough to Confront,* rev. ed. Regal Books, 1980. This book was one of the early volumes written especially for Christians. The author is convinced that confronting is a sign of caring. If people are not important, we will not care enough to confront them. Being passive and ignoring is a sign that we do not care. Augsburger provides many good suggestions about how to confront in a manner that is gentle yet honest.

Emmons, Michael L., and David Richardson. *The Assertive Christian.*

Winston Press, 1981. A minister and one of the authors of *Your Perfect Right* consider most of the traditional objections to Christian assertiveness. The authors discuss meekness, guilt, love, and responsibility. The book is thoughtful and clear.

Faul, J., and David W. Augsburger. *Beyond Assertiveness.* Word Publishing, 1980. In a sequel to *Caring Enough to Confront,* the authors propose two ideas, assertion and affirmation. When we assert ourselves, we level with each other. When we affirm others, we love them. The book offers numerous means for doing both at the same time. The authors contend not only that it is possible to assert and affirm but that this is the appropriate Christian way of living.

Jakubowski, Patricia, and Arthur J. Lange. *The Assertive Option: Your Rights and Responsibilities.* Research Press Co., 1978. This book contains some excellent techniques for becoming more assertive. It also offers many insights for reversing the negative fears and beliefs of nonassertive persons. Included is a useful test for helping to distinguish between assertive, self-effacing, and aggressive behavior.

Southard, Samuel. *Anger in Love.* Westminster Press, 1973. One of the earliest books on anger written by a pastoral psychologist, this is now out of print, but you may find it in the library. It reflects a keen sensitivity to the impulse to defend ourselves, coupled with an awareness of Christian teachings about love and forgiveness, and is an important addendum to the present volume. The author discusses the problems of hidden anger and the difficulty in being angry but not sinning.

For the Counselor

These titles are included for the professional who may be interested in the research and theory underlying the methods taught in this book.

Sanders, Randolph K. "The Effectiveness of a Theologically Oriented Approach to Assertive Training for Refusal Behaviors" (Master's thesis). *Masters Abstracts* 14:252, 1976 (University Microfilms No. 13-08786).

————. "Short-Term Assertiveness Training Among a Christian Population" (Doctoral dissertation). *Dissertation Abstracts International* 41:2345-B, 1980b (University Microfilms No. 80-28820).

————, and H. Newton Malony. "A Theological and Psychological Rationale for Assertiveness Training." *Journal of Psychology and Theology* 10:251–255, 1982.

Printed in the United States
1102800002B/487-507